TIME TO CHOOSE

God bless you,

Hilda F. Gutwein

Dawn E. Keßmeigal

TIME TO CHOOSE

*Growing Up under Hitler and
Watching History Repeat Itself*

DAWN KAZMIERZAK

WESTBOW°
PRESS
A DIVISION OF THOMAS NELSON
& ZONDERVAN

WestBow Press books may be ordered through booksellers or by contacting:

WestBow Press
A Division of Thomas Nelson & Zondervan
1663 Liberty Drive
Bloomington, IN 47403
www.westbowpress.com
1 (866) 928-1240

Unless otherwise noted, all scriptures are taken from
The Holy Bible, NIV version.

Scripture verses marked KJV are taken from the
King James Version of the Bible.

Any people depicted in stock imagery provided by Thinkstock are models, and such images are being used for illustrative purposes only.
Certain stock imagery © Thinkstock.

ISBN: 978-1-4908-3049-0 (sc)
ISBN: 978-1-4908-3048-3 (hc)
ISBN: 978-1-4908-3050-6 (e)

Library of Congress Control Number: 2014905186

Printed in the United States of America.

WestBow Press rev. date: 03/19/14

Dedicated to:

Jim and Ellie, without whom there would be
no book. Thank you for everything.
We love you.

The precious parents who are committed to raising the next
generation of godly thinkers and who will be intentional about
equipping their children with both a moral conscience
and the ability to self-govern so that they can be
citizens of a democratic constitutional republic.
Thank you, and may God bless you.

May God continue to bless the United States of America.

CONTENTS

ACKNOWLEDGEMENTS

We would like to express our gratitude to the following people and organizations.

The team at Westbow Press, for helping us to get *Time To Choose*, which was first published in 2012, back into print to continue getting its messages to audiences, who now, are even more eager to receive them, connect the dots, and act in virtue for our children and our nation.

To the Ludwig and Luisa Welker Family and the Gutwein Family, we are so thankful for you.

Thank you to the following people for adopting us:

- The Hope Missionary Church family
- The Jones-Hullinger family
- The Colonel Kenneth and Jan Grice family
- The Captain William and Patti Urosevich family
- The Max and Ellie Stroppel family
- The Dr. Clifford and Vicki Brooks family

Thank you to the following people and organizations for pointing us to secure attachment:

- Dr. Megan Spinks, thank you for calling attention to the emotion driving the behavior.
- Dr. Karyn Purvis and Dr. David Cross of TCU's Institute of Child Development, thank you for researching and for showing us how to nurture children from hard places.
- Focus on the Family

Thank you to the thinkers:

- Rabbi Dr. Reuven Feuerstein and Dr. Shmuel Feuerstein, thank you for acting upon the truth that man is created in the image of God, capable of immense neuroplasticity, and created to think. Thank you for your commitment to the Jewish youth of the Holocaust and your ceaseless efforts to teach all people to think and make wise choices.
- Dr. Jeanne Zehr and Dr. Cindy Gerard, who have "Soaring Minds." Thank you for your passion to see children and families thrive and for providing practical training on how to teach children and adults how to think. You teach one child at a time, one parent at a time. And, most of all, thank you for your friendship.

Thank you to the champions of freedom and truth in these United States:

- The men and women of the Armed Forces of the United States of America and the Veterans of each of these branches of the Armed Forces.
- Alliance Defending Freedom
- Answers in Genesis
- Family Research Council
- Charles W. Colson
- The Heritage Foundation
- The Constitutional Patriots
- And many more

Thank you and God bless you for championing the cause of truth and upholding the Constitution of our great nation. It is one nation under God.

PREFACE

One Nation under . . . Whom?

Flashback

My mom, Hilda, is a saint. At least, in my eyes she is. She's been my mom for over fifty years, and I can attest to the fact that she is one of a kind. My mom has this rock-solid faith in God. It's like she can reach out and literally touch Him. How did she get it? Well, you'll find out if you keep reading.

You'll also find out why she started having flashbacks.

My mom doesn't watch any war movies. She doesn't need to learn or read about war; she lived it. She grew up in a war zone. She lived under socialism, communism, and Hitler's nationalism. Then my mom and her family eventually immigrated to a land of freedom.

As you gaze into my mom's past, I believe it will open your eyes. You also will be challenged to consider these questions: If you were faced with similar circumstances in your country, would you and your family leave, and where would you go? Or would you stay, stand firm, and defend your homeland?

The time is now; it's your turn to choose.

Dawn Elaine Gutwein Kazmierzak

MAP

CHAPTER 1

What's a German Family Doing in Serbia?

My story, and the story of my family, begins way back in the 1770s, during the reign of Queen Maria Theresa (1717–1780) of the Austrian-Hungarian (Habsburg) Dynasty. The queen needed farmers, and she knew that there were farmers in Germany in need of land. The queen recognized that these farmers had the ability to transform the swampland in the Balkans into fertile land, so she made them an offer. The German farmers would be given the opportunity to develop this swampland in the Balkans into productive farmland. In exchange for this opportunity, when the land became productive, the farmers would be required to pay 10 percent of the value of each year's crops back to the Austrian-Hungarian government. This payment was termed "the land tax." The farmers would also be given the opportunity to purchase the land should it become productive and should their families desire to stay in the Balkans.

My ancestors formed a treaty with the Austrian-Hungarian government and moved from Stuttgart, Germany, to Crvenka (Tscherwenka, Rotweil), Yugoslavia (currently Crvenka Vojvodina Serbia) to transform this swampland into fertile farm ground. After the land became productive, my ancestors paid a 10 percent land tax to the Austrian-Hungarian government until they were able to fully purchase the land.

By the end of the 18th century, this area was colonized by Serbs,

Hungarians, and Germans. Through the farmers' hard work and perseverance, the land had become the wheat chamber of Europe. So, consequently, the neighboring nations wanted the land. In fact, this same region of the Balkan states is where the spark was ignited that eventually led to the First World War (1914–1918), after which, the Austrian-Hungarian dynasty was dismantled.

Starting in 1918, the town of Crvenka became part of the Kingdom of Serbs, Croats, and Slovenes, later to be named Yugoslavia. In 1918–1919, the town was part of the Banat, Backa, and Baranja region, and from 1918–1922, it was part of the Novi Sad County. From 1922–1929, it was part of the Backa Oblast, and from 1929 to 1941, it became part of the Danube Banovina. During this period, for a very short time, Crvenka was also under the communist oversight of Josip Tito.

I was born in 1932, to Ludwig and Luisa Welker. I was the youngest of eight children. I have a twin sister who was born a half an hour before I was born. With our arrival my parents now had four sons and four daughters. At the time of my birth, my father was an established, wealthy farmer who owned a significant amount of land.

As long as I can remember, I was in a war zone. Austria, Hungary, and Yugoslavia all wanted our land. Later, Germany wanted it as well. So we lived under the Austrian flag, the Hungarian flag, and the Yugoslavian flag, depending on which nation was in power at the time. As school children, we had to learn the language of the reigning government. So we spoke Hungarian, Serbian, Slovak, and our mother tongue, German.

From 1941 to 1944, Crvenka was under Axis occupation and was attached to Horthy's Hungary. Horthy Miklos had been an admiral in the Habsburg navy, and in 1920, he was asked to become regent, royal governor, and protector of the new Hungary. Horthy was styled "His Serene Highness the Regent of the Kingdom of Hungary." Horthy was not really a king, because the Hungarians did not want a king. A Hungarian joke sums it up: "For the next twenty-four years, Hungary would be a kingdom without a king, ruled by an admiral without a fleet, in a country without a coastline."

Horthy was regent from 1920–1944. He was adamantly opposed to communism and so, caught between two evils, he reasoned he could better manage Adolf Hitler. This strained alliance was finally broken when Horthy would not agree to Hitler's demands.

In 1944, the Soviet Red Army and Yugoslav partisans expelled the Axis troops from the region, and Crvenka was included in the autonomous province of Vojvodina, within the new socialist Yugoslavia led by Josip Broz Tito.

Since 1945, Vojvodina has been part of the People's Republic of Serbia, within Yugoslavia. At the end of World War II, many Germans left Crvenka.

Connecting the Dots . . .

Talk with your children about the various forms of government around the world and what has allowed America to become such a great country. (It is freedom.) As you study the various forms of government, be certain to clarify the terms, concepts, and context in which they are applied.

Next, explain how words like freedom, liberty, justice, and equality can take on different meanings when they are applied to various forms of government. The founding fathers of the United States applied these words when birthing our nation. These very same words—freedom, liberty, justice, and equality—are also used by the atheistic philosophies of Marxism, communism, and socialism, but in those philosophies, they can take on entirely different meanings. Highlight the importance of understanding the intended meaning of a word and its context before making any assumptions regarding any political platforms being promoted.

First-year cadets in the military academy are called "plebes." Plebes represent the slaves, or lowest life forms. Plebes are stripped of every privilege. A plebe can do nothing without asking permission from a superior and must do everything an upperclassman asks of him. A plebe must earn each privilege. This practice exists so that the plebe can grasp the immense cost and value of freedom. The soldier and officer must emotionally and physically value freedom's worth to the extent that he or she would be willing to die to preserve it in our nation. How much is freedom worth to you?

Think about it.

CHAPTER 2

Setting the Stage

Until I was twelve years old, we were a wealthy family. We had a home in town, with one maid who lived with us year around. We also had two farms in the country. The closer, smaller farm had a vineyard and an orchard. This vineyard farm had a house with a hired caretaker and a barn for animals. We made our own wine and took the grape musts to a distillery to make whiskey. The other, larger farm had a house and a big barn for horses and cows; a separate facility for pigs, which we raised for the market; and places for our chickens, ducks, sheep, pheasants, and peacocks. We also had a bunch of cats and dogs. There was a separate housing facility there for our hired employees. Two families lived there year around. Then during the harvest seasons, we hired thirty to sixty migrant workers to help out.

Our home in town had an enclosed porch on the front and side, floored with terrazzo, and a large, paved-brick courtyard, which served as a gated entrance for the wagons coming in from the street. This paved courtyard was separated from the back courtyard by another gate. The back courtyard was not paved. This unpaved back courtyard led to the stalls, where we kept the animals, as well as to a kitchen that was used for butchering animals and washing clothes. We had chickens, milking cows, horses for transportation, and a few mother pigs that needed close attention. We also had a vegetable garden and a few fruit trees.

The house had four bedrooms, two kitchens, a large pantry, a dining room, and a living room. It also had a partial basement, which included a cellar for produce and root vegetables and for fermenting sauerkraut.

We made lots of sauerkraut. The pantry upstairs stored all manner of smoked, dried, canned, and cured meats; the canned fruits and vegetables from our gardens; and the flour, butter, cheese, and milk. In the summer, these dairy items went into the basement. In addition, there was a complete attic, which was used for storing things, including the grains for the animals and fruit.

Mom often baked our bread, especially in the wintertime, because the heat from the oven would help to heat the house. The kitchen was large and included two ovens. The oven for baking bread was very large. Then there was a range, which also had a smaller oven. Mom would get up at 2 A.M. to start making the dough for the bread. The bread oven needed to be heated as well, but there was no automatic temperature setting. So, to determine if the oven was hot enough for baking, Mom would toss in a portion of flour. If the temperature was correct, the flour would burn immediately. I thought that was pretty cool. The bread would be done by 7 A.M., when we needed to leave for school.

Connecting the Dots . . .

Think about all the modern conveniences in our culture today. Have these timesavers increased our relational time with family and friends? Are the bonds of American families stronger today than they were in the 1930s? Why or why not?

Think about it.

CHAPTER 3

"What Will I Do Today?
Today, I Will Work!"

We were busy about the business of life, occupied with earning our daily bread and a little wine. My father was very production oriented. We would never ask the question, "What will I do today?" We all knew the answer: "Today, I will work!" And we would work efficiently, not wasting time or effort. There was always more work to be done. Even though we had hired help, we children had to work. My father's mottos were: "Never put off for tomorrow what can be done today!" And, "Never be late!" These two mottos have served me well for my entire life.

My father had come to a position of responsibility at a young age, when his father died. He was the oldest of eight children and helped raise his younger siblings. But it was my mother's family, the Kochs, who had the wealth. And it was my mother's inheritance that provided my father with his substantial start in farming.

During the school year, we younger children stayed in town. During the summer, most of us children lived at the large farm—unless, of course, we had an appointment with a doctor or had to go to summer school. I liked the farm, but I didn't like having to work all of the time. The older boys helped with the livestock and farming. The eldest daughter, worked with the hired help. She would assist in overseeing the crews we hired to help with the harvest.

We hired up to sixty workers during the harvest each fall. As payment, the workers received every tenth row of our crops. Only a small portion was paid in money. Payment for our hired help who lived on the farm year around was primarily with resources. They were given living quarters, a cow to milk, a pig to butcher, a chicken to raise, and a garden. In addition to resources, we did pay a small portion of their wages in cash so that they could buy the essentials that they needed. However, because they would drink away much of the cash, we paid mainly with goods. That way, we knew that they had food to eat.

We always had wine on the table at dinner, and we children were permitted to have a glass if we liked. It's funny, but I don't recall that any of us ever drank much of it. Since it was readily accessible, it was not that much of an attraction.

One summer, when I was five years old, we had just made wine, and Dad wanted me to learn how to fill his wine bottle from the casks in the cellar. We kept about six large, wooden barrels lying on their sides down there. I followed Dad downstairs. He showed me the opening on the topside of the barrel. This opening is where we would insert the tube portion of the siphon to draw out the wine. He placed the tube in the opening and demonstrated to me how to place my mouth over the mouthpiece of the siphon and suck up the wine. He then showed me how to hold my breath to keep the wine from flowing back into the barrel and how to pull the tube out of the barrel while holding my finger over the opening at the end of the tube. This prevented the wine from flowing back out of the siphon.

Next he showed me how to transfer the wine in the siphon to the wine bottle. This was a little complicated for a five-year-old. He let me practice, and I got to taste a little bit of the new wine. It was pretty good—much sweeter than what was usually on the dinner table.

Later that week, I got the big idea that I was going to practice getting the wine into the siphon and into a bottle. So I got a wine bottle and went to the cellar to practice. Well, there is a technique to this procedure, and while I practiced, I sampled more than my share of wine. In fact, I got so much wine that I fell asleep right down there in the cellar. I guess I was tipsy.

Dinnertime came, and I did not show up for dinner. This had never happened before because I liked to eat. My family was concerned. "Where is Hilda?" they asked. My entire family began to search for me and alerted the hired help to look for me too. They looked in the house, in the barn, in the sheds, and in the chicken coop. They looked everywhere. My dad thought I must have worked so hard that I fell asleep from exhaustion. So they kept looking in every possible area.

It began to get dark, and now they were really concerned. They began to wonder if someone had taken me. I was a very outgoing child and talked to everyone. They got out the lanterns and searched the property over and again.

Finally, the maid who was bringing the fresh milk down to the cellar tripped over something, or someone, on the bottom step of the cellar. It was me. She hollered, "I've found her! I've found her!" So they called the search party back into the house. Everyone was so relieved. And I was still tipsy. I couldn't understand why everyone was so worried. They put me to bed, and I slept really well.

The next day, everyone joked about my wine-tasting experience. And Dad never again asked me to go get his wine for him. My brothers would tease me about this for years to come. If I did not show up for dinner, the wine cellar was the first place they would start looking. I suppose that was one way of getting out of a chore. I still had to take care of the ducks, chickens, and the smaller pigs, and help in the house.

The large farm had a bedroom for the boys, one for the girls, and one for Mom and Dad. In the summer, when we were at the farm, my daily routine started with getting up, going to the kitchen, and talking to Mom. I would say, "Mom, what do you need me to do first?"

She would say, "I need corn cobs for the oven; then take care of the chickens and bring back the eggs. When that's done, I'll have a list of vegetables for you to get from the garden." Mom would hand me a cup of hot chocolate and a slice of bread with butter and jelly. I'd say my prayer and then eat my breakfast, grab my basket for the corncobs, and head out the door.

The weather was usually pretty nice in the early summer. I'd be dressed in some old clothes from one of my brothers or an old dress from one of my sisters. I'd get the corncobs and take them back to Mom so she could get the oven going to complete her baked goods for all the help. Mom would thank me and often request a bucket or two of water to be brought in for her to clean whatever entrée she was making for dinner, such as the chickens she had just butchered that morning. Mom knew I did not like to watch her catch and butcher the chickens, so she would warn me ahead of time or have it done before I was up.

After making certain Mom had what she needed to continue her plans, I'd head to the chicken house and start my chores there. I would check for eggs and take them back for Mom to use for baking. Then I'd grab a broom on the way back to the chicken house and start by sweeping the floor. I always hoped that their poop had landed on the floor. If they pooped in midflight, it could be all along the shelves. That was a lot more work to clean up. I'd put new straw on the floor and in the nests. Then I would clean out the water trough and put in fresh water. After that, I'd fill the grain trough and report back to Mom for the garden list.

With my garden list in hand, I'd grab a hoe and two buckets and head to the garden that paralleled the lane. The lane to the house was lined on both sides with fruit trees. We had cherry, peach, apricot, apple, and pear trees. The garden ran the entire length of one side of the lane. I would pick whatever vegetables Mom had on my list, wash them up, and take them back to Mom in the kitchen.

By that time, Mom was preparing for the noon meal, which was the largest meal of the day. I remember one day when we were having fried chicken. She already had the chickens butchered, but they still needed to be cleaned in hot water. That was why she needed the corncobs so that she could heat the oven to heat the water.

We did not have a lawn to mow at the farm. All the grounds immediately around the structures were a packed-solid surface so that farm equipment and other transportation would be able to drive on it easily. We called it a yard. Some of this surface was concrete, and most of it needed to be swept of leaves and debris, especially the sidewalks between buildings and the areas in front of the house, the barns, and the living quarters. If time permitted, I would sweep all of these areas every day. When I was done sweeping, it would be time for me to start setting the table for the noon dinner.

Dinner was served in the big dining room in the main farmhouse. We would usually have eight to twelve of us for lunch. Someone was always traveling somewhere and not in attendance. Any single, male workers would eat with us so that we would know they had had a good meal. Dad, who was up by 4 A.M. each day, had been working and supervising the hired help in the fields all morning and was always happy to sit down for the meal.

That day when we were having fried chicken, we also had mashed potatoes and gravy, cauliflower, and freshly baked bread. Dad had chicken soup for his appetizer. Then we had nut strudel for dessert. We children had water. Dad had a glass of wine. We also had fresh, seasonal fruit.

After dinner, Mom and Dad would take an hour of rest. The maid, my sisters, and I would clean up the dishes and the kitchen and complete the daily household chores. We would make butter and various cheeses, and then we would do the laundry, the mending, and the ironing until late afternoon. By 5 P.M., we would be starting the supper meal, and I would be repeating most of my morning chores: check the chickens, and get the water, vegetables, and items for supper. My sisters and the maid would be feeding and milking the cows. They would also feed and check the mother pigs and our personal stock of pigs. The hired men would see to the pigs we raised for sale on the market.

For our evening meal, we often would have cold cuts of meats, such as salami, liverwurst, *Braunschweiger*, and smoked bacon—from our own animals, of course. There were cheeses; pickled peppers and onions; beets; and fresh, homemade breads. We also had fresh fruit in season from our orchard.

If it was harvest time, supper would be another full meal like the noon meal. This might be goulash; *paprikash*; sausage and sauerkraut; pork chops; beef roast; and lots of good, homemade noodles or *Knödel*.

The typical harvest season sequence was wheat, rye, sugar beets, hemp, sunflower, and corn, which was last. Hay would be harvested throughout the summer. And like all farming, what we did depended entirely on the weather.

After supper, the kitchen was again cleaned up, the milk was taken to the cellar, and we would hope that we were done with chores. My last chore of the day was to check my chickens and be certain that their little door was latched to prevent a fox or a weasel from entering the chicken house. This happened one time; all my little chickens were killed. I felt so bad that I had forgotten to latch the door that I made an entire chick cemetery. I even made little crosses out of wood for all the residents and had a little service for them. While I was making the last cross, the axe slipped, and I cut my finger very deeply. I still have the scar. I found a cloth, wrapped my finger, and ran to the house. My parents were so kind; they understood how very sorry I was. They knew those chickens had been my pet chickens.

Later I overheard my parents' conversation. My dad commented to Mom, "Sorry about your chickens, dear."

She replied, shaking her head, "Ach, Ludwig, I think we put too much responsibility on this little chick."

As I got older, I also had to help take care of the livestock. I would need to let the cows out to graze the leftovers from the harvested fields. We had about twenty-five to thirty cows in the herd. I was responsible for helping to keep them where they were supposed to be. I specifically had to keep them away from the clover. If they got to that they would become extremely bloated, especially if they overheated. We had a dog that helped, along with a lead cow. If the cattle started going where they were not supposed to go, I would tell the dog to go get them, and the dog would go and nip the leg of the lead cow and redirect her.

Most of the time during our summers on the farm, we had a lot of work to do. However, we loved when it rained. Then we could play!

Connecting the Dots . . .

Entitlement programs did not exist in my world when I was growing up. Of course, everyone would work. If you didn't work, you didn't eat. People knew that. Those individuals who were physically unable to work were provided with support by other local people who knew them. Both parties kept each other accountable. It was a relationship of mutual blessing. This helping hand was provided in a manner that maintained the recipient's sense of dignity and self-worth. Whatever the individuals could still do, they would do well. People in need looked to God and to their neighbors, not to some government program. The government was broke, just like ours is today.

Today our leadership has created a whole dependent state within our nation. It is a form of abuse that has cost the recipients their dignity, independence, motivation, and sense of self-worth. Since the well-intended inception of entitlement programs, the ranks of participants have swelled to unfathomable proportions. As a result, these programs are breaking the backs of the ever-shrinking numbers of tax-paying citizens. These programs are strangling the economic growth of our country and the businesses that provide employment. And they are leaving an inheritance of insurmountable debt for our children. The system is not working; it is broken.

Make certain your children realize that government dependence is not an option. Help them to think about and to develop a plan for their future.

Think about it.

CHAPTER 4

Yuritsa and Fashion Trends

My two older sisters and I helped with all the work in the kitchen. We also helped with the canning; the laundry; the cleaning; milking the cows; and making butter, cheese, and yogurt. We bought very few items from the market. Some garden and orchard items were canned. Fruits like apples and pears were stored in the attic. Other items, such as carrots, potatoes, parsnips, cabbage, etc., were kept in a root cellar. Meat was canned, smoked, and some was made into hard salami or sausages that we kept in a cool, dry storage room. We were mainly a self-sustaining farm.

We bartered with the butcher, the baker, and the miller. Just as we paid our hired help with goods, that is also how we paid these businesses. We would take cows or hogs to be butchered, and the butcher would receive a portion of what he butchered as his payment. Since we had no refrigerator or freezers at the time, the butcher kept a record of how many kilograms of meat we could receive, and then we would go there and get the fresh meat we needed when we needed it.

At the large farm, we ground our own grain for the animals that lived there. The grain for the animals in town was ground at the mill in town. We took in corn and wheat, and the miller was paid with a portion of our wheat. He ground our corn and wheat into flour, which we took in bags to the baker. The baker kept a tab on how many loaves of bread we were able to receive from him when we needed it. He kept a portion of the flour we brought in as his payment.

We had very little time to relax and certainly no time to be bored. I never knew the concept of boredom. The boys had a ball and occasionally attended a movie. I had a cloth doll my sister made for me and one doll I made out of a corn stalk. One time, I actually made a whole furniture set for my doll out of green burrs. I worked on this project for a whole week. It must have been raining. I used a vine to be my little "playhouse" for this creation. When I was done, I showed it to my dad, who was so impressed and proud of me.

The next day, he sadly brought me bad news. An ornery cow had gotten out, found my secret hiding place, and trampled all of my special furniture. At that point, I decided to stick to my living animals instead of fake furniture.

At the large farm, we bred pigs for sale on the market. Sometimes we would have a piglet that the mother neglected to acknowledge. One such time, we children decided we would mother it. We named it Yuritsa. At first, we fed Yuritsa with a bottle. He followed us everywhere. We would feel a wet, little nose nudging our legs, wanting more grain or just a gentle pat and a kind word.

Eventually, Yuritsa was adopted by the cows and slept with them. But during the day, in hopes of some attention, he would follow us as we did our outdoor chores. We would save special food for him. One day, Yuritsa even made it onto the farm porch. We quickly shoed him out, but eventually we would let him lie down a bit inside there, careful that Dad did not catch us being so lenient. We would quickly hide Yuritsa if Dad was coming.

Of course, Dad knew that little pigs soon grow into big pigs, and children are going to get emotionally hurt if they develop an attachment to a pet pig. And we did. One day, Yuritsa was not to be found. We looked all over and could not find him. Later that week, we had pork for dinner. We were certain it was Yuritsa, so none of us children ate the meal. We would not eat any of the pork, bacon, ham, or sausage. Mom understood and gave the meat to the neighbors. That was the last pet pig we had in the house.

In the spring and the fall, a seamstress came to our home in town to make all of the clothing for the women and girls. The boys were sent to the tailor, who would take their measurements and then make their clothes. For the better clothes—coats, suits, etc.—we purchased the fabrics directly from the cloth factory and then provided this material to the seamstress and the tailor.

My eldest sister was beautiful and loved to wear the latest fashions. I always dreamed that someday I too would get to dress like she did. But, since I was the youngest, I usually would get hand-me-downs from my sisters. As I got a little older, the hand-me-down clothes did not always fit me. Being a little plump had its benefits; I got some new clothes. I decided that being chubby was a good thing.

One day, my eldest sister came home with a heavy scarf wrapped around her head. "Sis, that looks strange," I said. "Why are you wearing your scarf like that?"

She swore me to secrecy and then slowly removed the scarf from her head. "*Himmel Vater!*" I gasped. "What have you done?" She had gotten her hair cut short and had a permanent. And she had gotten her ears pierced. She was wearing gold earrings. This was a "no-no" in my parents' church denomination. There was no short hair, no jewelry, and certainly no piercing of body parts allowed. Oh dear! I knew that I did not want to be in the same room when my parents saw this new fashion trend in our home. But I was curious to see how it would turn out.

My sister put the scarf back on her head and went to Grandpa Koch. Grandpa was more lenient. My sister knew that if she could talk him into accepting her new look, it would influence Mom and Dad to accept it more easily too.

Grandpa loved my sister and understood the challenge and responsibility of being the eldest of eight children. With his wisdom, he advised her not to purposely draw attention to her new look. This meant that when church members were visiting Mom and Dad, she should just keep her head covered and not put in the earrings. This was great counsel.

My sister followed Grandpa's advice, and it worked very well. Mom and Dad accepted her new look, and we younger children got the benefit of our eldest sister paving the way for us to be a little adventurous too.

Connecting the Dots . . .

Style points! Review some fashion magazines with your daughter. Talk about the trends and who sets the trends. Discuss with your daughter what kind of message she wants to send about her character to those around her.

Conservative Muslim women totally cover their bodies because they do not want men to be tempted to sin because of seeing too much of them. That's extreme to us, but there is a lesson to be learned from it. If you advertise, you're going to get a response. It's no wonder so many unmarried teens find themselves pregnant.

Help your daughter to develop her own fashion taste, chosen thoughtfully, to transmit her desired message. More importantly, show her how to cultivate the inner beauty that is the most attractive attribute of any woman. Parents of boys will especially thank you.

Think about it.

CHAPTER 5

My Precious Mother

Proverbs 31 speaks about "the wife of noble character." My mom, Luisa, was a precious lady and fit this description. She was extremely efficient. My dad expected meals to be on the table at precisely designated times. He also requested that Mom have soup, at least for him, at every meal. To him, it was not a meal if it did not begin with soup.

Each day, my mom would tell us children what specific items to get or to set on the table. In a very short amount of time, she would have an elaborate meal prepared. Everything was made from scratch, no boxed mixes, and there were no leftovers. With ten to twelve people eating at each meal, we did not have any leftovers.

One time, I recall Mom looked at the clock, and it was already 10:45 A.M. We had not yet begun preparations for dinner, which was expected to be on the table at 12 noon. She had not even butchered the chicken yet! And we had to make the noodles from scratch. Amazingly, she got all of it done, and the meal was on the table by noon, with a bowl of soup for my dad too, of course.

In addition to managing and working in the households and seeing to meals and our personal schedules, my mom had to knit the winter socks, winter sweaters, and mittens for our family of eight children, our grandparents, Dad, and herself. She also had to keep track of all the live poultry. We had hens that would be sitting on eggs to hatch new chicks. All of these had to be logged because we would need to take care of the new hatchlings; the hens would not get off their nests to do so. Sometimes we would even stick duck eggs under the hens to hatch some more ducks.

My mom was never lacking for something to do. That is why I was so surprised one day when she made a special meal just for me. It was just the two of us out at the larger farm, and she asked me what I would like to eat. I don't recall my age, but I must have been pretty young because I answered that I would like "stuffing and hot chocolate." What a combination! If I had realized all the work, I wouldn't have asked her to do it, but she willingly did so. We gathered the eggs, bread, onions, celery, parsley, lard, butter, salt, pepper, milk, sugar, and chocolate, along with the husks to start the fire for the stove. And she went through all this work just for me. We enjoyed this special feast together, and I've never forgotten her special ways of demonstrating her love for me.

Another way Mom nurtured us was in helping my dad to understand that we were still children. My dad, who had to keep things productive, had a huge list of things that needed to be done each day. So after we completed one task, he'd have several more on his list for us to do. My mom would stand up for me sometimes and say, "Ach, Ludwig, let her rest."

Dad was very strict about the appearance of our home and properties. Everything had to look picture perfect: "A place for everything and everything in its place." That is a good motto, but it's hard to do when you are a child and in the midst of a project or homework assignment— or just in need of a break. So Mom would balance Dad's strictness about the appearance of the house and say, "Ach, Ludwig, they're just children; let them play a bit. I'll clean it up . . ."

My dad would worry, like a typical farmer, but my mom, with her calm, trusting spirit, balanced him perfectly. My mom was a thinker and had a terrific memory. She did not forget anything, it seemed, and could make thoughtful connections with all the information she gleaned. My dad would read to her as she was doing her chores in the kitchen. Whether it was the newspaper, the Bible, correspondence, applications, bills, catalogs, etc., she just filed the things he read to her away in her mind. Dad always consulted Mom before making any major decisions. She was his right arm. They really worked as a team. What a good example for us children.

I learned a great deal from observing my mom and other people. I learned to anticipate what would be needed next and to run and get it for her or for whoever needed it. Observing and listening—there was little time for talking, and little ones were supposed to be "seen and not heard." And, quite honestly, folks would sometimes forget I was there, so I heard a lot.

The skills of observation, listening, and thinking ahead would serve me extremely well throughout my whole life. God used them to help me adapt to all the new situations life would hold for me, especially in the United States when I did not know the English language well enough to ask about the specifics I was seeking to learn. So I watched, listened, and learned.

Connecting the Dots . . .

Moms and dads, do you realize how much your child watches you? Your children may not say it, but they can read you like a book. When learning how they should respond in various situations, children take their cues from you.

I'm going to step on some toes here. Moms, your "place" is with your developing children. Sure, it's much easier to work outside the home than it is to stay home with small children, but you should have thought of that prior to having children. The choice was yours. Now that you've made the choice to parent, you need to "do it properly", as Kipper, the British cartoon pup, would say.

Consider the message you send to your children as you drop them off at the daycare each morning. It's kind of like dropping off the puppy at the kennel. Wait until you're aged and your child puts you in an institution. Today your child may think, "Fine, Mom, you don't think I'm valuable enough to spend time with now when I need you. Wait until you're old and need me. So there!" What goes around comes around.

If you are a single parent or the primary breadwinner for your family, find a way to work from home, if it is at all possible. Seek out trusted family or church friends who will commit to helping you nurture and mentor your precious children. Your children are already at risk and need the extra assurance of a secure attachment to you. And you need the support of a faithful family. We all do.

Think about it.

CHAPTER 6

Formal Education and My Private Tutor

My early, formal schooling was in Crvenka. I began kindergarten at age five. In the German culture at that time, children were closely observed in kindergarten. This observation continued, and as they developed, the students were guided toward a curriculum that enriched their God-given, natural talents, abilities, and inclinations. After finishing elementary school, those students who planned to study at a university would attend gymnasium for grades five through thirteen. There were also trade schools and apprenticeships. Whichever educational path parents chose for their children, the graduates had a profession by the time they were eighteen years of age. With this profession, they could earn a living. Advanced studies at the university were also available.

I walked to school in town, went home for lunch, and returned for classes until mid-afternoon. I attended this elementary school in my hometown until I was ten years old. Then, at age eleven, I rode the school bus to Vrbas to attend gymnasium there. Elementary school was paid for by our taxes. But our parents paid gymnasium and university as private schools.

Our early schooling required lots and lots of memorization of poems from Göethe, Schiller, and other European authors. My sister, training to be a teacher, would read stories to us from *The Brüder Grimm* (*Grimm's Fairy Tales*) and other books. Penmanship was very important too. Our writing had to be beautiful and perfect. Math, history, science, art, etc. were also emphasized.

When I was just learning how to write, I had trouble making my number four. My eldest brother, Ludwig, would often help me with my schoolwork, especially if I would make hot chocolate for him. And I would; although, it was not instant. In order to make hot chocolate, I would need to start the fire again, get milk from the cellar, and get the chocolate, sugar, etc. I was little, so this was a serious investment on my part. I would finally have it done, and Ludwig would have his hot chocolate. Then I would sit at his feet with my little slate, and he would teach me to make my little-chair fours with a missing leg.

I always loved to watch Ludwig draw and paint. He was a very good artist. He was ten years older than I was and was sharing an apartment with other students at the university. But he still came home on weekends. I was the adoring youngest sister and would tag along after him when he was home. I'd polish his boots and make him hot chocolate, and he would give me little assignments to do.

On one occasion, Ludwig agreed to paint a picture for me. "Okay, what would you like? I'll do a watercolor for you," he said.

I wanted the painting to be full of colors, so I opened my arms wide and replied, "A big basket full of vegetables."

Ludwig tilted his head, arched his eyebrows, and nodded his head. Then he smiled and replied, "If you go gather all the vegetables." So I ran out the door.

This was in the early fall. I went to the garden and cut the cabbage and turnips and picked the pepper and tomatoes. Then I dug up the carrots, parsnips, potatoes, and beets. The vegetables were filthy, so I had to go draw water from the well to wash them and then polish them with a rag. I did this while mentally kicking myself and thinking I should have chosen a bouquet of flowers instead. It would have been much easier and just as colorful.

Ludwig created the most beautiful painting of vegetables I could have imagined. He added many more colors and a few items I had not even gathered. *Hmmmm*, I wondered to myself, *maybe he could have just done the entire painting from his head anyway. Either way, next time, I will think before I give him my choice. Maybe I could choose a castle and see what he would have me gather then.*

Ludwig could make me laugh. We would have family relations or other visitors come to our home. Of course, we children were to be polite and well mannered, and we were to show respect by staying close to honor our guests. One time, some cousins came for a visit. We were sitting in the periphery of the room, and Ludwig began to sketch the couple. This gave me something to look forward to because we could not hear the conversation but needed to be present. When Ludwig held the completed sketch up for my approval, I nearly burst out laughing. My cousin was short and plump, and her husband was very tall and skinny. Ludwig had really exaggerated these physical features with some liberty. It was pretty funny. Of course, we did not share the humor or the drawing. But his attention to me made me feel it was a special privilege to be his little sister.

Ludwig was attending the university. I always assumed he was studying to be a teacher because he was my teacher. But I'm not really certain what degree he was working toward. He certainly had a gift for working with children, especially with his little sister.

When Ludwig was of age, he volunteered for military service, and he never returned home.

Connecting the Dots . . .

If your children are in public school, do you really know what they are being taught? When was the last time you spent an entire day with your children at school or read their textbooks? What do you know about the social pressures they face or are exposed to at school?

If you are serious about parenting your child, consider a school where the curriculum meets your family's values and priorities for education, a school that teaches your child to think and prepares him or her to succeed in the future.

Think about it.

CHAPTER 7

What's Yours is Mine; and I Want It.

Let them know what the king who will reign
over them will do. (1 Samuel 8:9)

The land in which we lived was very fertile, as I mentioned earlier. It was situated between the Danube and the Tisa rivers (see map in chapter one), just north of where these two rivers intersect. The land was well watered and ideal for agriculture. Its location was also ideal for transportation and industries, such as milling, that relied on water. As a result, all the surrounding nations wanted this land, and those nations were willing to fight for it.

As a result, our land often came under the authority of a new government. Whether it was the Hungarian government, the Yugoslavian government, the Hungarian government again, or the German-Axis control during World War II, the new government always would require us to share our personal property with the incoming country's military. (Currently, as of this writing in 2012, this land is situated in the Autonomous Province of Vojvodina, in the West Backa District of Serbia.)

During these changes of government, for periods of up to three weeks, we personally provided housing for military foot soldiers as well as for cavalry and their horses. The horses were stabled in an enclosure at the rear of our property, where hay, straw, and water were accessible and provided by us. This area was dirt but had been packed solid by many years of wear and did not get muddy with inclement weather.

The military did provide their own food rations as well as their own military cooks. Their cook-supply wagon would be positioned in our front courtyard, which was paved with bricks.

The soldiers slept in our enclosed terrazzo-tiled porch, which encompassed the front and some of the side of our home. They brought their own bedding and were very respectful—except, in my mind, for one officer who slept in our master bedroom on one occasion. This officer actually propped his booted legs on the table in that room. I was shocked! As children, we never would have dreamed of putting our feet on the good furniture like that.

My dad had told me about some of his World War I experiences, when he was serving in the Austrian-Hungarian military and said that things like this could happen, but I never thought I would witness this happening in my own home! I knew how much time the maid and the ladies in my family had to spend keeping the picture-perfect appearance of all the furnishings and accessories. So it really bothered me that these military men, in their soiled garments, could just plop down on our couch as if it were a pile of hay somewhere. But I got over it. What choice did we have?

My mom made dozens and dozens of homemade yeast donuts for the soldiers. One time, seeing the huge quantity, I remarked, "But, Mom! All this?"

She thoughtfully replied, "Maybe someone will do this for your brothers." I didn't understand at the time, but I would understand later.

People knew that war is war, and if the government had need of anything that someone had, the government could claim it for its purposes. The government could conscript our sons, our daughters, our horses, our produce, our wagons, our home, our property, and even our brand-new Mercedes Benz automobile.

My father had just learned to drive and had purchased a brand-new Mercedes. The car was only a few weeks old. Then the German military quartermaster came and said to my father, "Herr Welker, we need your auto." He followed that with a big speech about how valuable the auto would be to the national security of our country and about how we should be proud to have the honor of sharing our goods this way. (That was the typical speech they gave when they came to conscript our goods.) The quartermaster then gave my father a receipt and told him that after the war, he could claim whatever had been conscripted . . . if anything was left to claim.

I felt so sad for my father. He had been looking forward to riding in an automobile instead of on a horse or in a horse-drawn wagon. He had just gotten to ride in the car a few times. I had ridden in it twice, but it was no longer meant to be.

This conscription of our property taught me another valuable life lesson, particularly about ownership. We really never "own" anything. It's all just temporary and on loan for us to use. All of this stuff can be taken away at any time. It's just stuff, and I learned not to place too much faith in it. I learned to place my faith in my heavenly Father.

Connecting the Dots . . .

Recognize that a government has no resources, no money of its own, except that which it takes from its people or that it has borrowed or taken as spoils from another source. The government redistributes this as it sees fit and does so to gain the allegiance of the recipients, who relinquish their own freedom in exchange for dependence on the government, the central power.

The government does not produce any tangible product by which a profit is gleaned; its only product is bureaucracy. It is a huge monster with an insatiable appetite. It does not even create employment. Employment is created by free enterprise. Make certain that your children grasp the significance of these concepts.

Think about it.

CHAPTER 8

Laying the Solid Foundation

Train a child in the way he should go and when he is
old he will not depart from it. (Proverbs 22:6)

Amidst the national instability, my parents had a solid faith in Jesus
Christ. My father taught my first prayer to me while I was sitting on
his lap when I was about three-and-a-half years old. I had been asking
Dad who Jesus is because my Grandpa Koch had always said, "Look
to Jesus." So my father taught me the same prayer I would teach to my
child: *"Ich bin klein, mein Herz ist rein, kann niemand drin wohnen den
Jesus alein."* "I am little, my heart is pure; no one can live in it but Jesus
alone." My first song was, *"Weil ich Jesus Schäfelein bin, Freue ich mich nun
immer hin. Über seine guten Hüten wehr mich schön weiss zu bevirten. Der
mich liebet, der mich kennt und bei meinem namen nent."* "Since I am a little
sheep of Jesus, I'm always happy. Because of His perfect life, He can
lead me right, who loves me and knows me and calls me by my name."

At this time, all children were, by law, required to take instruction
in catechism from one of the three accepted churches of the state. The
accepted churches of state were the Catholic, Lutheran, and Reformed
churches. The priest or reverend would come to the school and teach
the students there during the regular, daily class schedule. A 10 percent
tithe was required from every family, whether they went to church or
not. This was the church tax.

My parents were members of a Christian church that was not an
accepted church of state. So most of my siblings and I attended the

Lutheran catechism classes at school and attended the Lutheran church services. My parents applied their Christian faith through their daily walk of life, and they taught us to live according to the Good Book. So in this respect, I had a fertile Christian heritage.

Connecting the Dots . . .

What's your family's spiritual training plan? Please don't say that it's the church Sunday school programming or the youth group. That's like saying that your weekly grocery visit is responsible for keeping you healthy. It's not the church's responsibility to train your family. It's *your* responsibility. You are the parent.

Understand that it doesn't have to be sitting down for a daily drudgery of Bible stories. Most church-going children know these stories by heart. But that's part of the problem. In our culture, the word "story" has taken on the meaning of "fairy tale." As a result, children are often left thinking that the Bible is merely a collection of nice fairy tales. We think, *After all, those stories were for people living in the Dark Ages, right? We are much more enlightened.*

Young minds reason, "I'll go to church with my parents because I have to, but I am looking to science and technology for my real salvation. Who knows, maybe they'll clone me." We live in two separate worlds, one fairy tale and the other real. They are nicely compartmentalized, with no overlap.

Unfortunately, the church has failed to address theories of humanism touted as proven fact in our government institutions and media today. And as a result of the church's silence, children are left to assume that it can't address them. But the Bible is dynamic; it's alive, and it's relevant to today. Since you are the parent, you need to take the lead here and show your child how very accurate the Bible is. Expand upon this and make it relevant to the world in which your child lives. Meet your children where they are. Address the pseudo-science, evolution and origin theories that saturate the media, textbooks, and movies in our culture. Train your child to be a thinker and not a blind follower.

Think about it.

CHAPTER 9

Hitler Youth and the Indoctrination of Young Minds

It is taught that whoever controls the media and the education controls the nation.

In 1934, Hitler became dictator in Germany. At that time, I was two years old and, of course, did not think much about it. Initially, Hitler did some good deeds to gain a following. He added assistance programs for the poor, created programs to heat homes, and began educational programs, such as Hitler Youth. Then as Germany continued to annex other nations and promote Hitler's dream of a Third Reich, we began feeling the effects in the Balkan states too.

As time went on, our land of Vojvodina, Serbia, Yugoslavia-Hungary, came under German occupation. The government was in an uproar. There was no freedom of speech or press and no objective information. The majority of us had no idea what was really going on in the world. With no truthful sources of outside information, we were essentially brainwashed due to the propaganda that was being fed to us.

Young children and youths of all ages were indoctrinated into Hitler's propaganda. In our town, as in most towns under German influence, children were enrolled into Hitler Youth. Most children were enrolled by six years of age. I was enrolled at an older age because my parents were not in favor of it. I did not want to join it, but some of my older brothers were attending the gymnasium and university, where they were exposed to Hitler's propaganda. They, like many young students, were swept into the charismatic presentation and promises. These were promises of hope and a prosperous future for a new German nation. They rallied on the side of my joining it too.

When Hitler appeared on the world stage, Germany was still digging out of the losses of World War I and was very susceptible to this self-confident, motivational type of leader. Hitler was a very energetic, dynamic, and charismatic speaker. He made promises and offered hope that things would be much better for the new generations of Germans. To the young people in university or gymnasium, Hitler seemed to bring a breath of fresh air, a newness of energy, and the opportunity to redeem the nation from the shame of World War I.

My father tried to counter these influences and reason with my brothers, but often youths fail to recognize the wisdom of experience. And, unfortunately, youths tend to repeat the same errors of history. As a child, this was hard for me to observe since I loved both my parents and my brothers.

I recall overhearing a conversation between my father and my eldest brother, Ludwig. I am sure they did not realize that I was listening, or they at least didn't think I could comprehend the meaning of their heated conversation. We were in the kitchen at our home in town. The main kitchen, as in most homes, was the center of family activity. With thirteen people living in our home, someone was always in the kitchen. There was a long dining table in the center, which was where we children did our homework. Mom was making noodles over at the side work counter. She was always working and listening.

Ludwig had completed the highest age level of Hitler Youth and had absorbed some of the mindset. The next step in Hitler Youth was to join the military forces, which he did. He was wearing his Hitler Youth uniform, bearing the markings of his highest rank. He and Dad were sitting at the end of the long table. I came into the kitchen to do my homework and took a seat (unnoticed) at the other end of the large table. Ludwig was passionately verbalizing to my father some of the latest decrees of the Hitler propaganda regarding the Jewish people. He was becoming more animated with each new phrase.

"It's the Jews. We need to be rid of them. They've polluted the country long enough." He banged his clenched fist on the table. "Look what they did before. We're still bearing the shame! Don't you see it? Don't you understand?"

My father gazed into Ludwig's eyes and said, "I do understand, Son. Be careful whom you believe, and be careful what you say. Remember, we too are Jews in Christ."

My brother, denying his catechism confirmation, definitely did not want to accept that, in Christ, we too are Jews by adoption. Ludwig shot up from the table and countered emphatically, "No way do I have Jewish blood in me!" He then turned his back on Dad and, with large, manly strides, stormed out of the kitchen. My dad watched my brother leave the room and shook his head in sadness.

I took in the scene and was also filled with grief. I loved my father and knew he was right, but I loved my precious brother also. Ludwig was my special teacher. This attitude I saw in him was why I did not want to join Hitler Youth. I preferred to stay home and do chores instead of go to learn this type of divisive teaching, teaching that was tearing my own family apart.

Within two years, my three eldest brothers had joined the German army. Their enlistment was called a *Frie Must*, a "volunteering" but with little real choice. If my brothers had not enlisted and served in the military, our family would have been shunned and viewed as traitors to the Fatherland. My father was excused because he was a farmer, and the country needed the food. We also had to raise certain additional crops for the government, such as hemp to make ropes, castor beans for castor oil for medicinal purposes, and sugar beets. Those were not our usual crops.

Eventually, it became necessary for me to enroll in Hitler Youth. Ludwig told my parents that people were asking why I was not in attendance. "Where are those twin sisters of yours, Ludwig?" people would chide. For a long time, our excuse had been that my twin had asthma and my parents did not want us to be separated. But this excuse was no longer accepted. I had three older brothers serving in the military, and our absence was no longer an option. So now, my twin and I had to participate in the Hitler Youth programming.

Initially, Hitler Youth looked very much like Girl Scouts or Boy Scouts do today. Girls had uniforms comprised of white blouses, black skirts, white knee socks, black shoes, a black scarf with a scarf ring bearing the Nazi insignia, and a cap designating our specific level of Hitler Youth. The boys' uniform was similar; they just had pants instead of a skirt.

My level of Hitler Youth met once a week after school, except if we were being trained for a special performance. "Performance" meant parading for special military generals. These formal dress parades increased in frequency as time progressed and the fighting grew closer. The older-aged levels of Hitler Youth met regularly in the university and gymnasium towns. From what I gathered from overhearing my brothers talk, Hitler and his dream of a new Third Reich were pretty much the focus of most conversations among their peers. Hitler's ideas had become their hope for the future.

The leaders of the Hitler Youth would stage a customary meeting for my level at the Heim, the town clubhouse. Boys and girls had separate meetings. The parents were not in attendance, and most parents did not know what we children were being taught. Most of the fathers were serving in the military. The meetings included a pledge of allegiance to the German nation and marching songs about Germany. And there was a lot of propaganda that they wanted us to embrace. Of course, it wasn't labeled propaganda; it was cloaked in nationalism, family, and historical "facts."

The Hitler Youth leader would stand at the front of the assembly and shout *"Sieg!"* (Win!) Then we youth would lift our right arm in the air and respond *"Heil Hitler!"* (Hail Hitler!)

We would then march a high-step march, saying, *"links, – rechts, – link, – rechts"* (left, right, left, right), keeping in step to the marching music or chant. We always had to be certain to begin the march with our left foot, or we would be admonished with a shout: *"Links fuss erst,"* which means, "Left foot first!" If we got off on the wrong foot, sometimes we could shuffle and get back in step without being noticed. But if we got caught out of step, we would get pulled out of formation. Then we would have to march all by ourselves for a kilometer. While marching alone, we were required to continue saying, *"links, – rechts, – links, – rechts . . ."* while moving our corresponding arm up and down and stepping with our corresponding foot. We had to do this while the rest of our group went on with the scheduled agenda for the meeting. This meant that sometimes they would go inside and leave the marching child all alone outside with an instructor. I remember this because I had to do it—all by myself. A kilometer was a long march for me to do all by myself when I was still young. I can't forget that experience. Those propaganda strategists knew that fear is an extremely effective motivator of memory.

We would also have to say phrases like, *"Heute gehört uns Deutschland, uns Morgan die ganze Welt!"* ("Today Germany belongs to us; tomorrow the entire World!") And we had callisthenic-type exercises and did more marching. We did a lot of marching.

In addition, we were required to memorize lots of propaganda about Hitler. Specifically, they wanted us to recite lines about his life and all of his accomplishments. We also had to memorize propaganda about the high-ranking officers in Hitler's regime. We were required to memorize all of this information and pass verbal testing on it. The testing was nerve-racking for me because I did not want to have to remember those things. It just did not resonate well with my young mind and my Christian upbringing. This propaganda included many accolades to men as if they were gods. I knew they were not gods; they were just men with big egos who had a hunger for controlling other people.

Whoever orchestrated the propaganda was a master at making it effective and well embraced. They knew how to weave it with emotion and family attachments. They also knew that if we repeated something often enough, or heard enough other people saying it, we would begin to believe it as truth—even if it was not truth.

For Mother's Day, we put on a program. The entire venue was packed. It was rare for parents to attend our performances. Usually, the military personnel were the only observers of our performances. Most fathers were not around since most men were serving in the military somewhere else.

For that program, we had to memorize a very tender-appearing poem and recite it for our mothers. The girls' poem was about how our mother gave us the greatest thing by teaching us to speak our native tongue, German. The boys' was about a young man's return after serving in the military to defend the motherland, Germany. It spoke of how joyful it would be for this son to return home to his mother and recount all of his military experiences to her.

These meetings did not settle well with my conscience. We could not talk about them at home because of the hired employees. We lived in an area of so many varied nationalities and such a long history of conflict. Everyone had ears, and we did not know where each worker's allegiance was. Conversations could be used against our families or us if we expressed an opposing view. So we had to attend these Hitler Youth meetings. We had to perform at the dress marches and keep our mouths shut. We had to do what was expected of a good German family.

All the while, I was closely observing the unspoken language of glances and the countenances of the faces around me. I was always listening, but I was not openly showing that I heard something that maybe I shouldn't have heard. Certainly no one was repeating it or asking any questions about it. Many topics we just did not discuss.

Connecting the Dots . . .

From what source do you receive truthful world and national news? Can you discern truth from propaganda or biased information?

Propaganda is successful because of the massive number of times a child or individual is exposed to it, and the multiple sources from which one's senses are bathed in it. Without intentional parental mediation, a young child does not even detect the error. Then the child begins to accept absolute falseness as being true. Think about ways you can help your child weed through all the propaganda he or she hears and find the truth.

Think about it.

CHAPTER 10

Defeat Deception with Truth

While the Hitler Youth movement was feeding us this propaganda, God was making sure I was fed the truth. He especially did this through my dear Grandpa Koch. The truth of God was wrapped in the nurture of my loving grandfather.

Grandpa Koch was my mother's father, and he treated my father as a favored son. Grandpa and Grandma Koch lived with us in our town home. They had their own living areas within our house. That was just what German families did back then. They would build or add on to their homes so that all members of the family could continue to be together. Each family member had his or her own part to contribute, and that contribution would change as each person aged. As my grandparents aged, it became their mission to pass on to us children the wisdom and truths that they had learned.

It was never considered a burden, but rather an honor, to have our grandparents right there with us. Grandpa taught me how to pray, read the Bible, and sing German hymns. He also taught me the value of everything.

Grandpa was a well-known man in the community since his father had been a judge. I remember that Grandpa had a long ledger book with a list of many people who had borrowed money from him. When he learned that they were having hardship and could not easily afford to repay him, he would just cross their names out of the account book and forgive their debts. To me, these acts seemed just like what God does for us.

Since Grandpa and Grandma Koch lived in the same home we did, as often as I could, I would sneak over to sit at Grandpa's feet. I say "sneak" because Mom did not want me to bother them all the time. My grandma needed to rest, and Dad usually had chores for me. But I loved my grandpa and cherished the times I got to spend with him.

Now, I must confess that my mom did have valid reasons for reminding me not to "bother" my grandparents. Grandpa and Grandma Koch's living quarters were right there in our home. And this living area provided a great sanctuary for me to escape to and get to play. I had learned that "being out of sight and out of mind" from my dad had its benefits. If I stayed clear of Dad's path, he would not see me and assign me yet another productive task.

Grandpa and Grandma's living area included a large, rectangular room. This room was furnished with couches; chairs; a big dining table; grandpa's big, overstuffed chair; and an adjoining kitchen. Off to one side of the room, there was a coal-burning heating unit. The unit had pipes arching out from both sides, and it kept the room very warm and comfortable. It also had a heating cubbyhole about a foot wide that had a flat surface. This flat surface in the unit could be used for heating small containers. This was ideal for heating small portions of coffee, soup, or anything else that would fit in a small container.

The heating unit sat about three feet out from a long wall. This space provided just enough room for my twin and me to have a rectangular-shaped play area. One end of our "play area" was a wall. The long wall and the heating unit itself formed the sides. The other end was where Grandpa Koch's big chair sat. Grandpa sat there as our sentry. He was our guard and watchman. We were off to his right-hand side. He could see us and what we were doing, but no one else could see us. This was perfect.

Grandpa, from his pivotal location, could see Grandma Koch on her couch. But Grandma could not see us in our play area. Pointing to the hidden play area, she would regularly ask Grandpa, *"Was machen die Kinder?"* ("What are the children doing?")

He would answer, *"Ach, die sind spielen . . . sind ganz gut."* ("They are just playing; they're doing fine . . .") What more perfect location could we ask for?

One afternoon, during Grandpa and Grandma's *"Ruhestunde"* (rest hour or nap time), my twin and I decided that there was one more benefit to our play area, when we recognized the perfect opportunity to try out our newly acquired candy-making skills. Earlier in the week, our Aunt Barbara had demonstrated to us how to make simple hard candy. She had showed us how to take sugar, vinegar, and a dab of baking soda and form a delicious sweet treat. My mom was not thrilled about our having this new information and had specifically told us not to make any candy when we went to Grandpa and Grandma's. But now, presented with this perfect opportunity, we were overtaken by temptation and reasoned that no one would ever find out. We would eat the evidence.

My sister and I gathered the few necessary items and used the surface of the heating unit to cook our confection. We made our candy, cooled it, and had our own little feast. Sweet success! Or so we thought.

While we were swallowing the last piece, Mom appeared. "Kinder, what are you doing? Did you make candy?" she asked.

"Oh no, Mom," we lied, and smiled, showing the candy still stuck in our teeth.

We were caught. The smell of burnt sugar was permeating the entire house, and our remaining supplies were still lying about. But our Aunt Barbara, Mom's older sister, came to our defense. She confessed that she had provided the sugar. She took the blame herself and made Mom promise not to discipline us for the incident. But the act was cataloged in Mom's permanent memory file, and she soon had more evidence of my tendency to get into mischief. This next episode, I would rather forget.

The barber would regularly come to our house to use his barbering skills on Grandpa Koch. The barber would bring all the interesting items of his trade and lay them out on the big table in Grandpa and Grandma's living area. We got to watch this. He would put a big cape on Grandpa. Then he would trim Grandpa's hair with his scissors. Next he would paint lots of foamy shaving cream on Grandpa's face with a big brush. It looked like so much fun. Then he would take his blade and run it up and down a big, leather strap.

The next part was so intriguing to me. The barber would take the blade (it just looked like a curved dinner knife to me) and run it along Grandpa's face to scrape off the cream. I liked how the barber did this with great precision, as if he were carving a statue out of the cream. He would create the sides of grandpa's face, sculpt his chin, and then carefully carve out Grandpa's mouth. Sometimes he would pluck Grandpa's eyebrows, ear hairs, and nose hairs too. I wasn't sure how I felt about that part. But I wanted to try doing the creamy carving part. What fun it would be to get to play with foamy cream and create a beautiful masterpiece.

I waited patiently, and one day, I knew it was time to test my skills. The barber had been to Grandpa's, and he had mistakenly left some of his tools. This was great! All I needed was a willing participant. Who could be more perfect than my previous co-conspirator? My twin!

I presented the opportunity and all its obvious benefits to her and worked to convince her of my extensive knowledge of the profession. After all, we'd watched the barber do this to Grandpa many times. What could be simpler? She wasn't an easy sell, but she finally consented.

We had the area to ourselves. Grandpa was sleeping in his bed, and Grandma was over in Mom's big kitchen, talking to her. So I began to put the remains of Grandpa's recent barbering, which were still on the table, to good use. "Waste not, want not."

I directed my twin to take a seat on the chair at the table. I applied the remaining shaving cream to her face. Then I took the barber's shaving tool with the curved handle and began to work on my masterpiece. I carved the foam from her cheek and then proceeded toward her mouth. Then, oops, my tool slipped.

The next thing I saw was blood. I was scared to death. My twin looked at me. She was ready to cry. I grabbed a towel and pressed it on her lips and begged, "Please don't cry. I am so sorry." We ran to our hiding place behind the heating unit. The blood had seeped through the towel, so I grabbed a pillow from Grandpa's chair and took off the case. I used the pillowcase to apply pressure to my twin's cut to stop the bleeding.

Finally the bleeding stopped. I whispered to my twin, "It's going to be okay, Sis. I think it's stopped bleeding. I'm going to take off the pillow case and the towel, so hold really still so I can check."

As I was removing the bloodied fabrics, I heard Grandma coming in. That was not good. As she walked in and surveyed the room, she said out loud, "Those two are too quiet. What's going on here?" She looked

in our hiding place, and we were caught. She assessed the situation and said, "Let's go to your mother."

We quickly went to Mom, who was in the big kitchen. Grandma said to Mom, "Here are your two troublemakers. See what they got into this time."

Mom sat my twin on the chair and looked at her lip. Then she asked, "What were you thinking?"

I recounted what had happened.

Mom said, "Hilda, you never should have done this, and don't you ever try this again."

I promised her that I would not.

"But you did keep yourself calm, and that was a good thing. It was also good how you applied the pressure to the wound to stop the bleeding. And God's hand was in this, how the edges of the wound are joined so nicely. There will be a small scar, which you both will remember. But I thank God that you are both okay."

I think my mom went easy on us because she realized that those tools should not have been left out on the table and within our reach. She realized that we were just young children, eager to emulate those around us.

I appreciate my mom's thoughtful parenting and her recognition that it was never my intention to harm anyone. My mom metered out just the right amount of admonition for me. I am thankful for her abilities to consider all the variables and nurture me in the way that was best for my tender spirit. This accident was another stepping-stone in my learning to better think through my actions. I am reminded of it every time I see my twin.

Sorry, Sis. Thank you for forgiving me.

Connecting the Dots . . .

Consider all the variables that contribute to your children's behavior before you mete out any consequences. Let your children take the lead in doing what is right. Give them time to do and say the right thing on their own initiative. Practice makes permanent. Be their coach and not their warden.

Think about it.

CHAPTER 11

Poetry with Visual Imagery and Timeless Truths

In the summer, we all ate together on the porch. One day, when I was about five years old, dinner was called. I was the last one to arrive at the table. I knew I was late and that they had already prayed. My food was already dished out on my plate. So I quickly took my seat beside Grandpa and started to eat. He smacked my hand and said, *"Ver ohne gebet, zu Tische geht, an ohne gebet wieder aufsteht, sieht dem Oxen und Esel gleich, hat keine teil am Himmel Reich,"* which means, "Whoever goes to the table without a prayer and gets up from the table without a prayer looks no better than the ox and the donkey and has no part of the Heavenly Kingdom." What a sobering picture. Never again would I begin eating without first thanking God for His provision. I sure did not want to lose my part in God's heavenly kingdom!

It is the German way that timeless truths, declared by a respected mentor, will speak their messages for a lifetime. While we know that God really is not that severe, what Grandpa said and did was the German way of getting the point across, the point being that we should remember that everything we have, even our daily bread, comes from our heavenly Father. It is only fitting that we always make it a priority to stop and thank Him for His faithful provision for our every need.

My Grandpa Koch was a good teacher, and I hung on his every word. I knew that whenever he admonished me, it was because he loved Jesus and he loved me. I also understood that he had gleaned a great deal of wisdom throughout his life. Grandpa Koch filled a vital role in our lives by being able to mentor us with time, focused attention, listening ears, and godly wisdom. He would read to us from the Bible. And when we were old enough to read, he would have us read the Bible to him. Then he would explain the meaning of what we were reading. For various reasons, I think children today are missing this vital mentoring from their grandparents. Perhaps we are all witnessing the results in our culture.

My parents had eight children and were very busy with all the responsibilities of daily living and managing the properties and workers. Amidst these demands, and the uncertainty of our country, they did not usually have time to sit down and teach us one-on-one, so they found ways to do this throughout our daily lives. I must say that although Dad made me work, he also balanced these demands with relationship.

My dad and I had a solid attachment. I knew that he loved me. When the occasion would present itself, he would say to my mom, "Luisa, I'm going to go visit the Lelbach's and take Hilda with me. Get her ready, *bitte.*" Then my mom would tell me which dress I should wear, and I'd quickly be ready to accompany my dad. We'd take a horse-drawn wagon and go visit neighbors or church friends. The men would have a glass of wine as I watched and listened.

One time Dad even took me with him to our family vault at the cemetery. Mom reminded Dad that I was still pretty young and to be careful about what I saw. The vault was in a large, underground room. The workmen were sinking the caskets of my ancestors to make more room for the next generations. I thought it was interesting, but I really did not understand why it was necessary to make more room. We were all pretty young. Yet I understood later.

In the afternoons, my dad would go inspect the fields, garden, orchard, or vineyard. He wanted to see what needed to be done next. Often he would take me on a walk through the garden and quiz me about which plant was which. This was challenging, as I also had to distinguish these new sprouts from weeds. Some days we'd take the horse and wagon and go inspect a more distant field. He would point out all the various plants to me and then quiz me later as we passed by a similar crop.

One time we walked by a field and I said, "Oh, what beautiful wheat. It looks like we'll need to harvest it early."

Dad turned to me and said, "What did you call that?"

I said weakly, "Wheat?"

He replied, "Look again, child; that is hay."

I had a tough time distinguishing the hay, oats, and wheat when they were still young. Dad had me look closely and find the differences, and I got better at identifying all the vegetation in its various stages of development.

My dad gleaned great benefits from making the effort to strengthen our relationship. I developed a great deal of respect and honor for him. I don't think my dad had the opportunity to spend so much time with my older siblings. But since I was the youngest of the eight, I think I received the benefit of his many years of previous parenting. I am thankful that Dad let me be his little companion.

Connecting the Dots . . .

Does your child have a secure attachment to you? Our culture continues to promote constant activity; yet very little of this activity is truly relational. We have lots of technology but little face-to-face communication.

Now there's a topic: "communication." What has happened to communication in our families?

An entire chapter could be written about the negative impact that the "smart phone" is having on our culture. What has happened to our ability to organize our thoughts and to think before we speak? Watch what people do with their smart phones. It can be hilarious. It's obvious that for many people their phones have become an addiction. Grandparents complain that when their grandchildren come to visit, they don't even look them in the face. The children are so absorbed in their media device that they don't even engage in conversations. Perhaps they don't know how.

People are rarely "present" in the current moment. Their minds are often thinking about the next topic or the next event on their schedules. So, what is it about face-to-face relationships that are so important anyway?

The human infant is totally dependent at birth and is truly not mature enough to be independent until the latter half of the second decade of life. Why? We were created for relationship. We were created for secure attachment to our parents. We were created to be in a stable family unit. This foundation of a secure attachment is what develops the child's ability to self-regulate.

This ability to self-regulate, to think, is vital in a democratic republic. If a people cease to be able to think and control themselves, if they cease to be intrinsically motivated to do the "right" thing, then they will require an external source to control them. It is happening.

Think about it.

CHAPTER 12

The Reason Why

I remember one particular summer day at the farm when I was twelve years old. My older siblings and all the hired workers were already out in the fields. They were harvesting the sunflower seeds, which were used to make sunflower oil. When ripe, the sunflowers had to be harvested as early as possible or else the seeds would fall to the ground and the birds would eat them. The sunflower plants had very rough leaves, much like corn and the plants were quite tall. The harvester had to grasp and cut off the head of the plant without shaking all the seeds out of it. Thankfully, I was too short to help harvest the sunflowers.

My dad came running into my room early in the morning, just as the sunlight was trying to peek through the curtains. He tore the covers off of me, saying, "The cows are out! Go after them!"

I knew what that meant. I hastily threw on my brother's shirt and pants, along with some shoes that were much too large for me to wear. Then I ran for the door. My mom quickly gave me a piece of buttered bread with jam on it as I left the house.

Once I was outside, I ran through the stubble from the harvested wheat fields, hoping that the cows had not yet made it to the clover. As I rushed through the stubble of the wheat fields, the thorns from the berry vines under the wheat remains tore at my ankles. I could feel the thorns and burrs slicing my flesh and the blood beginning to ooze. The debris was sticking to my open wounds, but I couldn't stop because I had to catch those cows.

It was early, the air was heavy with moisture, and there was still dew on the grasses. The clouds began to darken, the air was thickening, and it smelled like rain. Trying to catch the cows in the rain would be even worse.

I ran for about ten minutes, panting to catch my breath. At one point, as I was running, I lost a shoe. I had to go back to get the shoe because the vines, stubble, and burrs were cutting my feet.

The sky continued to darken, the wind picked up, and I knew we were in for a storm. After quite some time and, thankfully, before the cattle had gotten to the clover, I was able to reach them. I led them back, still keeping a hurried pace, trying to reach the corral before it began pouring rain. I got them all in the corral just as the first raindrops hit me.

Despite my success, I was extremely upset and very angry. Usually I did not get that way, but I was fuming. I had blood dripping from my legs, ankles, and feet, and the cuts were caked with all sorts of burrs and dirt. I was hot, stinky, sweaty, and crying—I was such a mess.

When I walked to the porch with bleeding feet and sore soles, my mom saw me and asked, "How did things go?"

I replied, "I have the worst dad anybody has ever had. How could he do this to me?" I don't recall any other time when I responded so rudely to my parents. Normally, I honored them.

My mom's response was something to the effect of, "Wait until your dad finds out what you have said."

I looked at her questioningly and asked, "You won't tell him I said that, will you?"

She sympathetically nodded her head and said, "*Mein Kind*, my child, you know I will need to."

I was a miserable wreck the entire day. I went about my chores, hoping and praying that Mom would change her mind—or, better yet, forget. But Mom never forgot anything.

All during dinner, I kept watching my parents, trying to overhear any passing conversations or subtle glances. When dinner was finally over and it was time to clean up, I thought that just maybe I would escape any discipline. Then I overheard Mom tell Dad what I'd said. "But Ludwig, look at her, go easy on her, *bitte*," she interceded.

I knew that I was in big trouble because Dad told me to come into his office. I was scared to death, but I went. I was ready for a big whipping. I was twelve years old, and I had never received a whipping from my dad. With dread, I went into the office.

To my surprise and horror, Dad was really kind to me. He very nicely said, "Sit down."

Oh, I thought, *I'm in bigger trouble than I even expected to be.*

He sat down in a chair, faced me, looked me in the eyes, and said, "I love you. I love you very much. That's why I'm doing what I'm doing. I spent seven years in the military, including World War I. I want to teach you how to work and how to do things so you can defend yourself and be ready if war comes and you have to do so." He knew that we were on the brink of war even then. He wanted me to be strong.

I told him that I was sorry and asked him to forgive me. I am sure he did because this incident was never brought up again. He really was a great dad.

I left his office, went out to the chicken house, bawled my eyes out, and prayed to Jesus, asking Him to forgive me.

Connecting the Dots . . .

Talk to your children about your responsibility as their parent. Share with them why you teach them the things you do and why you require certain behaviors from them.

How often do you look your children in the eye and tell them that you love them? Is their preciousness reflected on your face? Do you make eye contact with your children in most of your conversations? Do you stop what you are doing, walk over to a child, look him or her in the eye and parent him or her up close? Try it; it works.

Think about it.

CHAPTER 13

Eventually People Recognize the Truth

During World War II, my eldest brother, Ludwig, was stationed in Finland. In August of 1942, while he was searching for land mines, one exploded and hit him on the right temple. He was killed instantly.

As we were reading the telegram that detailed his death, Grandma Koch came in and wondered why we all were crying. She took the news really hard because Ludwig was one of her favorite grandsons. She died in November of 1942, just a few months after receiving the news. It was also very hard on my mother, Luisa.

We later received a package containing Ludwig's personal items. This package contained his journal. I remember my dad reading aloud the journal to my mom and our family. One of Ludwig's journal entries said, "*. . . das ist ja Wahnsinnige, was wir dulden müssen von unserem Führer!*" ("This is crazy what we must tolerate from our leadership!") Ludwig then detailed how he and his fellow soldiers, while stationed in Finland, had to regularly strip down to their underwear, take an axe, walk down to the frozen waters, and cut through the ice. They would then have to swim in the frigid waters. This was to make them tough.

When I heard this, I was shocked and saddened to learn what hardships my precious brother had had to endure because of his tender youth so easily trusting in a charismatic leader. But as we later learned of the atrocities of Hitler's leadership, we were thankful that Ludwig had died so early in his military career. Hitler's horrendous directives did not match with the character of our brother.

From Ludwig's journal entries, we were certain that he had come to acknowledge the evil of Hitler's agenda, the truth of my father's counsel, and the counsel of his Savior—a Jew. Others recognize truth, but it is often too late.

Connecting the Dots . . .

Parents, you have a tough balancing act. You want to respect your child or young adult's budding independence. Your goal is to mentor your children to become their own people. But when do you teach that truth that you have gleaned from your own observations that your children may not want to hear? How much will you regret later if you don't put voice to your insights?

Some day they may thank you. Truth that is planted will still bear fruit. Take heart that although you may not see the results of your efforts to teach your children, the message can speak for itself. The Holy Spirit will do His work. You do yours.

Think about it.

CHAPTER 14

Going Home and Leaving "Home"

I will lead the blind by ways they have not known, along
unfamiliar paths I will guide them; I will turn the darkness into
light before them and make the rough places smooth. These are
the things I will do; I will not forsake them. (Isaiah 42:16)

Things continued to worsen politically. The war was coming closer,
which was forcing our family to make a decision about what to do and
where to go. That was the question of the day. Should we stay or leave?

Grandpa Koch became very ill. His poor health made our decision
to stay or leave even more difficult. However, God made the decision
for us. He took Grandpa Home in June of 1944. I was twelve years old.
That was the last funeral I attended in my hometown. It was so hard
on me because he was my mentor, my best friend, and my pal. I would
run to him whenever I had any troubles. So now where would I go?
He had taught me many German hymns and taught me the Bible and
the importance of serving Jesus and Him alone. I would do as he did; I
would go to Jesus in prayer.

After Grandpa passed away, we kept Grandpa's body in a casket
in our house for twenty-four hours. The funeral was held in our home.
I remember walking down the stairs, holding onto my father's hand.
When I saw the casket, I started crying. Then I looked up through the
windows and saw the most beautiful rainbow in the world.

My dad said, "Look. He's at peace. He's Home."

That was the good-bye and closure I needed. Grandpa was at Home and at peace, and I had to go on.

The doctor who had attended him, also a friend, told my mother, "You will soon envy your father because times are looking very bad."

We had little knowledge of what was going on the national or world scene except for what the government wanted us to know. We had no telephones, no computers, no televisions, and only a few radios. The radios didn't work half the time because of poor reception. There was not even a newspaper in our small town. Few sources existed for us to get news, and what was given to us was rarely truthful information. Whenever there was news that the government wanted us to have, a drummer would be stationed every three to six blocks. He would beat his drum so that the people would gather around him, and then he would read the "news" aloud. Most of what we did receive was strictly propaganda to accomplish Hitler's agenda. The people were afraid to speak, because those who did speak out sometimes disappeared.

Eventually, the military started gathering up our Jewish neighbors and friends. It was then that we realized how ignorant, misled, and brainwashed we as a people had become. We had been so busy, so occupied with the daily struggles of life, that we were blind to the twisted agenda of the government leaders. By this time, most of the men between the ages of sixteen and fifty-five years of age had been drafted into military service and were no longer at home to protect their own families and properties.

It was an awful experience to witness this roundup of our Jewish neighbors. They were taken to the Heim a few blocks from our home. The Heim was the town clubhouse that also served as the town hall. I remember seeing them lined up against the walls. The Jewish citizens were instructed to hold up their arms and a leg and not to move a muscle. If they moved, they were kicked or hit with a club. We were all in shock.

I don't know how long they had to stand there because I ran home, crying all the way. When I got home, I threw up all over a good rug we had. Then I had to figure out a way to clean all that up. What an awful day. We dared not talk about this at home because of the hired help as well as the increased military presence in our town and the very real possibility that we might need to house them. Those Jewish people were our friends, classmates, and neighbors. What was going on? This was not right!

The Jewish people were then forced to wear a Star of David armband, and we had to wear one with the Hakenkreuz-swastika. I hated this. The Jewish business owners and homeowners had to place the Star of David symbol with the wording *"Jude,"* on their homes and businesses, designating their heritage. We were told to boycott them. Their businesses were defaced, and many were closed due to lack of income. They wanted to leave, but they were not permitted to do so until they were forced to do so later—under military guard.

Through this time, even as a young girl, I learned that no matter what happened, God was in control. The song *"Eine Festeburg is unser Gott"* ("A Mighty Fortress is our God") became very dear and a great anchor for me to hang onto. God is our refuge, and He is with us whatever may come.

I still had two brothers in the military, Konrad and Eduard. Ludwig had already been killed in Finland. My brother Konrad was stationed in Austria, close to Zell am See. My brother Eduard was stationed somewhere in the Russian zone, but we didn't know where.

Since the war was coming closer, our family had to make a difficult decision: whether to stay where we were or to flee our land. If we stayed, we were taking the chance that after the war we would end up in Russia. We did not want that. We preferred to end up on the American side. So we decided to leave.

Connecting the Dots . . .

This is a difficult one to stomach. People often ask the question, "How could those German people follow a leader like Hitler? How could they participate in Hitler's Holocaust of the Jews? How could they commit the unspeakable atrocities to fellow human beings? How could they merely stand by and do nothing?"

Are you any different? Are we as a nation any different? How are Hitler's Holocaust and the responses of the German people any different than our own nation's holocaust of unborn children? Have we too become blind to the truth, like the German people? Are we too concerned with our status and our stuff, with our own self-preservation, that while we lazily graze on the lies of humanism, we can somehow justify the brutality of our own actions? When did we stop thinking?

It's your turn to choose.

Think about it.

CHAPTER 15

Shifting Sand, Solid Rock

It was the summer of 1944, and I was twelve years old. I was at the farm with my mom and my youngest brother. My brother and I were cleaning out the cow barn. We heard Dad's horses and wagon coming up the lane. He had just taken some pigs to the market in Crvenka, so we were expecting his return to the farm. As he stopped the team in the yard, we came out from the barn, and Mom came from the house to greet him and see how things went.

Earlier that morning, after Dad had left, Mom had shared some thoughts with us in the house. We were sitting in the dining room, finishing our breakfast, and Mom said, "Something is wrong. I don't know what it is, but I have this overwhelming feeling that something bad is going to happen." Mom had expressed this same type of intuition just before we received the news of my brother Ludwig's death.

My brother and I said, "We sure hope not, Mom. We hope the boys are okay." We had not heard any news from Konrad or Eduard for quite some time now, so the well-being of our brothers in the military was always uppermost in our thoughts. We hugged Mom and went to do our chores in the barn. Neither one of us liked cleaning out the cow barn, so we wanted to get it over with.

After Dad arrived home in the wagon and Mom reached the wagon, she looked up at Dad and said, "Something is wrong, Ludwig, isn't it?"

Dad was climbing down from the wagon. He said, "It's bad. It's very bad news."

"Did we lose one of the boys?" Mom asked with sorrow.

Dad shook his head. "No, as far as I know, they are okay. But we have to leave home."

"When?" Mom asked.

"Now," he replied.

Dad turned to us and said, "Children, get your things together."

"What?" we asked, just starting to process what this would mean.

"Important things," he answered.

I started to cry. I thought of all the things that were important to me: my animals, my doggie, and my friends. All of these things were important to me, but I couldn't take any of them with me. I knew I couldn't take any of my animals, so I thought at least I could take my brother Konrad's saddle. Konrad's doggie had died while waiting for him to return to the farm. And at least I could take his saddle for him. I brought the saddle out to put it on the wagon.

Dad and Mom were still standing by the wagon. They were having a conversation about what Dad had learned in town. They had not gotten very much cash from selling the pigs, and Dad knew that since we were leaving, we would never receive the remainder of the money. Most of our assets were in property, and some were posted as credit on our accounts at the various businesses in town. Since most things were done by bartering, the sale of the pigs was one way we could obtain cash. We also kept our own savings because we did not use any outside bank.

I walked up full of tears and was trying to lift the saddle to put it in the wagon. Dad looked at me and said kindly, *"nein, mein Kind, wir können das nicht mit uns nehmen."* ("No, my child, we cannot take this with us.") I just laid the saddle down and walked away crying.

I went to the house, cleaned up, and changed clothes. I took some dresses off the hangers, trying to find something important and portable. Most of our good clothes were in town anyway. I picked up the doggie, gave her a hug, and handed her to the maid. I kept crying. Walking in a flood of memories, I took the dresses to the wagon. I was still trying to grasp what was happening. Was it *really* happening?

Mom got the cash box, a few photos, and a small satchel. We all climbed into the wagon, overwhelmed. We were lost in our own thoughts. We kept slowly turning our heads, stopping to rest our eyes on a specific site, as if to fix it in our minds' eyes. We were recounting a flood of memories, events, and conversations we associated with each spot. The farmhouse had been built in 1936, and all of the other buildings were newer than that. The large commercial hog house was only two years old.

I can't begin to fully comprehend how my mom and dad must have felt as we pulled down the lane. They were leaving behind so many of their hopes and dreams. Some of the fruit trees were bearing fruit, which would soon be ready to harvest. We had planted them all. The garden was all up, as if eager to promise a good yield if we would stay. Dad and Mom had worked so hard to provide this heritage for their children and future generations. They had even planted walnut trees for us to use for our furniture when we got older and started our own families.

That was the end of my life on the farm. We were refugees, but we would find refuge in Christ. The Psalmist wrote, "I will take refuge in the shadow of your wings until the disaster has passed" (Psalm 57:1).

We did not talk much on the one-hour drive into town. My brother and I kept looking at each other, still trying to grasp if this was for real. We got into town, and my dad sent my eldest sister back to the farm. When we left, we had not told the maid why we were leaving. So my sister went back to keep order at the farm until Dad had fully worked out his plan. His main concern at this point was how we could all travel. Although we could begin by wagon, it might be necessary to walk on foot, depending on the terrain or available food for the horses. This would be very difficult for my twin. Many families were in this same situation, having to decide what would be best for their children.

Since my twin sister had severe asthma, my father decided that the two of us should go with the Hitler Youth. Like most Socialist-Nationalist ideologies, there was this vision of a New Man who would create a New Order that was purged of all impurities. Hitler's vision was of a racist nature, the Jew-free, Aryan utopia. We young Germans in the Hitler Youth were to be that new Aryan race. So in order to save the seed, we were to be transported away from the war zones and continue our training to become the hope of tomorrow. In Hitler Youth, we would travel by train and not go by wagon or by foot. Since my twin and I were members, this was an option.

Dad went down to the Heim, gathered all the details, and registered my twin and me to travel with the next available group that was leaving. The train would be departing in two days. My mother was allowed to pack one suitcase for the two of us. She packed two dresses, an extra pair of shoes, socks, underwear, hankies, a slip, and toothbrushes for each of us. Then she made us a little snack bag with honey cookies and a sandwich wrapped in a cloth napkin.

Those two days were filled with constant activity. Many people were leaving and trying to figure out what they should do. People were coming in and out of our home, wanting information from Dad. Dad had served in the military for seven years, including during all of World War I, and he was a leader in the community. Folks wanted his perspective on what they should do. We did not have any time to privately sit down and talk things over as a family.

Throughout this time, my mom was a calming influence on us all. My father was always concerned about something. It was his nature to worry. But my mom, with her solid foundation in Christ and her trusting spirit, would steady him with her unwavering faith. With all those townspeople bringing their anxieties, her Anchor held firm and set the tone for the rest of us. Our faithful heavenly Father would continue to care for us all. I took my cue from her and knew that I too would need to be a calming influence for my twin and those we would be traveling with on the trains.

Soon it was time to leave the house. My dad and my brother were going to take my twin and me to the train station. Just before we stepped out onto the street, Dad took us aside for a parting word in private. He looked us in the eye, held our hands, and said, "Children, remember what you have been taught. Remember to look to Jesus. And remember, although everything else will be left behind," and he emphasized as he motioned with his hands, "no one can take away what is in your heart and in your mind." Dad paused and promised, "If there is any way possible, I will find you."

We hugged our mom and walked out onto the main street. I never did get to say "good-bye" to my eldest sister, who was still at the farm, or to my other sister, who was attending a private school and not yet home.

As we walked down the street, my brother and my twin walked

ahead of Dad and me. Dad quietly said to me, "Remember, take care of your sister."

I promised to do my best.

We got to the train station, hugged our brother and Dad, and boarded the train. We took our seats on the train and waved good-bye to Dad and our brother. We did not know if we would ever see our family again. That was the last time that I would see my hometown of Crvenka.

Connecting the Dots . . .

Would you and your family be mentally prepared if you were faced with the decision to leave your home and all of your things behind?

This is scary stuff, and no one wants to think about it. But believe me, your children are thinking about it. Children today are far more aware of what is happening in the world than many of their parents are. Children have relatives fighting in the Middle East. They are flooded with horrific scenes on the nightly news and play video games with the same themes. Some young people may even recall 9/11. Oh yes, that did happen, didn't it?

Be open to discussing these events with your children, as is age appropriate. Provide practical counsel, and ultimately, point your children to the One who will be their Anchor through it all.

Think about it.

CHAPTER 16

"Let Us Run with Perseverance the Race Marked Out for Us"

We took the passenger train from Crvenka (Tscherwenka) to the neighboring town of Vrbas. While we traveled, we had with us German foot soldiers who were carrying guns as our protection.

In Vrbas, more people joined us, and they put us onto freight trains to protect us from air raids. The enemy attacked passenger trains, but they did not attack freight trains as often. The boys and the girls were separated, so only girls were on our train. The car in which I rode had just had horses in it. We could still smell the ammonia from the horse urine. The workers simply threw down straw to cover up the refuse.

From Vrbas, we traveled to Budapest, Hungary, where we went through an air raid. We had to evacuate the train. We were all on the side of a hill, lying down. While waiting there, I saw one of the biggest shocks of my life. A group of SS Schutzstaffel (Protection Squadron) soldiers came along, leading a group of Jews, driving them like a large herd of cattle. The SS soldiers were fully armed with guns and clubs. If any of the Jewish prisoners stopped or fell down, the soldiers would hit them with their clubs.

Below the hill that we were on was a large cabbage field. When the group of Jewish prisoners reached that area, it was like a swarm of locusts. The Jewish people were so starved that they wolfed the cabbages down. I remember that the only things left in the field were the stubble and the stems from the plants. Everything that was edible was gone from that field.

We went back into our train. All of us were very upset and crying. The guards tried to help comfort us.

Connecting the Dots . . .

Why do so many people pick on the Jews? This is a question we all must ask ourselves. What is it about the Jewish people that is so significant? What is it about them that annoys other people? Starting at the beginning, let's consider the following thoughts.

Do you ever ponder what the current world would be like if Abraham and Sarah had obeyed God and waited on His timing? What would "now" be like if impatient Sarah had not taken matters into her own hands? But she did not wait. She talked Abraham into having a child with her handmaid, Hagar. Abraham consented, and Ishmael was conceived. Ishmael is the father of the Arab nations.

Hagar eventually was kicked out of the camp, and the angel of the Lord told her, "You shall name him Ishmael [God hears], for the Lord has heard of your misery. He will be a wild donkey of a man; his hand will be against everyone and everyone's hand against him, and he will live in hostility toward all his brothers" (Genesis 16:11–12).

Sarah and Abraham then followed directions, and Isaac was born. He was the child of promise. Isaac would be the father of Jacob, Israel. And after the exodus from Egypt, Isaac's children would be known as the Hebrew nation, the Jews.

Surrounded by nations that worshiped hundreds of various gods, the Hebrews formed a covenant with the one true God at Mount Sinai. They were given the Ten Commandments by God, and the Hebrew people were instructed to have no other gods but God—no bowing down to any other idol or image. They were given laws about their relationship with God and relationships with other people. The sign of this covenant was circumcision, to provide a constant reminder to this covenant people of their relationship with God.

Throughout history, the Jewish people have, at times, wavered in their obedience to the laws that God gave them. These laws were given to point the Jews to a dependence on God as their King. At each point of wavering allegiance, God would warn them and call them back. Many times God delivered them from foreign domination. They had a truly unique relationship with God, one that was enjoyed by no other nation. The Jews were and are God's chosen people. They were the nation through which the Messiah came.

Over time, the Jews would eventually accept their special relationship with God. They would learn to rely on God for their protection. They would, with fervor, obey the laws of the covenant. These laws were designed to help them recognize the Messiah when He appeared on earth. The Jews learned to bow to no other gods but God. Even Alexander the Great honored this cornerstone of their faith. Alexander permitted the Hebrews this privilege of continuing the practice of their faith as he expanded his empire. His treatment of the Jews and his tolerance of their religious practices set the stage for many centuries to come.

This not bowing to any man, king, or Caesar is what has earned the Jews the reputation of being an unruly people. They will not compromise on the cornerstone of their faith. God is their King. The Shema, "Hear, O Israel: The LORD our God, the LORD is one" (Deuteronomy 6:4), is the Jew's creed.

The Jewish mind is trained to think, and it is brilliant. The Jewish mind is trained to consider all of the options and develop new strategies. This tiny nation, placed by God in the location He chose, had to develop skills to survive. At the juncture of three continents—Africa, Asia, and Europe—along valuable trade routes, the Jewish people have spent much of their time in the middle of a war zone. They've had to maintain their identity; pass on their traditions; and learn how to adapt through numerous government conquests, exiles, repatriations, shifting politics, and the diaspora. As I said, the Jews are thinkers and have been blessed with keen minds. They have a love of life and an undying will to survive as a nation. And they will survive. It's in the Book.

No totalitarian form of government, whether it be socialism, communism, fascism, or a dictatorship, will long tolerate a people who both think and refuse to bow down to its leader or leaders. These types of governments want submissive sheep that will allow themselves to be led to the slaughter for the government's greater agenda. It's about control, and the Jews are not about to be controlled by external force. They will fight for the survival of what they know is God's directive to their nation.

Scripture tells us, "Let us fix our eyes on Jesus, the author and perfecter of our faith . . ." (Hebrews 12:2).

CHAPTER 17

New Families, New Foods, New Mittens, Same Manners

From Budapest, Hungary, we went to Wiener Neustadt, a suburb of Vienna, Austria. Prior to our arrival, the local people of Wiener Neustadt had been informed that a group of refugee children was coming from Hungary and that each family was required to house and act as foster parents for one child until other places could be found or conscripted for the children to stay.

Once we got to Wiener Neustadt, we transferred from the trains to military trucks and were taken to the courthouse square. The local people chose children from the group, but no one wanted to take in two children, so my twin and I were separated.

The lady who chose me was the Bürgermeister's (mayor's) wife, Frau Dietrich. She asked me why I was so sad, and I told her, "My father told me to take care of my sister, who has asthma, and now we are separated. I don't know where she is."

She said, "I will find out where she is and see if I can help you." She was a wonderful lady. She treated me like her own granddaughter.

The very next morning, when I woke up, she already had news. I got to the kitchen and Frau Dietrich was on the phone and she said, "I found your sister. I am going to get her, and she will be with you by this afternoon."

Thank You, Jesus!

The people who housed children were given an extra ration ticket to

help feed them. However, the family that housed them had to purchase
the food with their own money. The ration tickets gave them permission
to purchase only a specific item in a specified quantity, if that item was
available at the specified time. They still had to pay money to purchase
the item.

Having the resources to purchase any item was a significant
consideration since the prices continued to escalate as supplies grew
fewer. This encouraged a huge black market industry. Even the water
was rationed!

The families were also given clothing ration tickets for the children.
My sister and I did not have hats or mittens, and it was very cold during
that time. As soon as she became aware of our need, Frau Dietrich
placed an order for mittens and hats for us.

I was thankful for the training my parents had given me. After
we had been living with the Dietrichs for a few days, Mrs. Dietrich
commented, "You come from a good family."

I was pleased and asked her why she said that.

She smiled and responded, "When you entered our home, you
showed respect. You took off your shoes, you hung up your coat, and
you kept your belongings in order. And you willingly offer your help to
me throughout the day. Your mom would be proud of you."

That taught me that if I always left things better than I found them,
I would be welcomed to return. When a child doesn't have a home or
know where her family is, that is a big concern.

The Dietrichs owned a furniture business. The business was on the
ground floor, and their living quarters were upstairs. At the time when
we were staying with them, they were also housing their daughter-in-
law and their four-month-old granddaughter, as well as Mr. Dietrich's
mother. Their son was serving in the military. So the house was full.
I think again of how gracious the Dietrichs were to take us into their
home and pay for our needs, especially when they already had taken in
their son's family and Mr. Dietrich's mother.

One evening, we were in the kitchen. It was a large, well-
apportioned room with beautiful, handcrafted furnishings and lots of
colorful decorations. We were all seated around the dinner table, having
just begun the meal, when the phone rang in the business downstairs.

It was the Dietrich's son calling, so all the family went to listen and speak with him.

Thank goodness the family left the room. I had been watching my twin, who was turning green. As soon as the family left, she promptly vomited on the bench and the floor. It was fish soup. Oh dear! We had tried to be so polite and eat what was put before us, just as our parents taught us. But my twin could just not stomach the soup. Now what should I do?

I quickly searched around for something with which to clean up the mess and finally found a baby diaper on the radiator. The diaper would work. I wiped off my poor twin and cleaned up the mess. Thank goodness she had missed the tablecloth. "Now, how am I going to get this smelly stuff off of the diaper?" Water was rationed so I could not use any of the water. The bathroom was just off of the kitchen, so I quickly ran into the bathroom and washed the diaper out in the toilet bowl. I kept washing it until it looked, felt, and smelled better. At least the fishy odor was not so strong. I hung the diaper cloth back on the radiator to dry and quickly took my seat back at the table. I smiled at my twin, who still looked pretty green.

The Dietrichs returned and shared some news about their son. They were so glad to hear from him and relieved to learn that he was alive and well.

Grandma Dietrich soon noticed that my twin's soup bowl was empty. She excitedly commented, while clasping her hands, "Oh, my dear, I am so glad you like the soup! It is my absolute favorite. It is considered a delicacy, you know. I raise the turtles myself. They are kept in the bedroom you are sleeping in. I only feed them fresh vegetables, chopped so they can digest them well." She went on in more detail about the special turtle diet. "Isn't it just marvelous? You must have a second bowl."

I looked at my twin as if to say, "Don't you dare take any more!"

My twin grinned sheepishly and politely said, *"Danke schön, aber ich habe genug."* ("Thank you kindly, but I've had enough.") We really did think it was fish soup. It smelled like fish, and it sure did not taste like chicken! So now we had to add turtle soup to our list of items to avoid.

This dinner took place just after we had been paid that high compliment on our manners. I think I told Mrs. Dietrich what had happened so that she would not waste grandma's special meal on us children who could not appreciate its appeal . . . and to save the turtles.

While we were staying with the Dietrich family, we still had to take classes at school. Since the camp there was overflowing with children, we had no classrooms. We were given our assignments to complete at home.

We stayed with that family for about five or six weeks. Then the orders came that we refugee children had to leave. Since Herr Dietrich was the mayor, he had some knowledge regarding our new destination, but he could not disclose this information because it was to be held secret. After all, we Hitler Youth were to be the new Third Reich. Herr Dietrich knew that where we were going would be cold, so he did encourage his wife to call about the mittens again. And she did.

The night before we were to leave, Frau Dietrich received a call from the store that our hats and mittens were in. But it was too late to go to get them that night. So the next morning, as Herr Dietrich was taking us to the station, Frau Dietrich ran into town, hoping and praying that she could get the hats and mittens before our train left.

Just as we were boarding the train, she came running, yelling, "Wait! Don't close!" In each hand, she had a set of mittens and a hat—one for my twin and one for me. She gave them to us and then hugged us each good-bye.

Years later, my dad found out that Herr Dietrich was the only Bürgermeister who was not executed after World War II.

Our train took us to Neustadt an der Tofelfichte in Czechoslovakia (now Czech Republic). Upon arriving, we again transferred from the trains and onto trucks. Then, when we arrived at our destination, we again went to the courthouse square.

Just as before, there was no room in the camp there for our lodging, but there was room there to school us. So, just like the Dietrichs had chosen to house us, a dentist's wife chose us. She liked my twin, so she picked her. But when my twin was picked, she told the woman, "Ma'am, if you take me, you also have to take my twin."

The woman looked at me first and then replied, "I guess I can handle that."

We stayed at night with the dentist's family, but during the day, we stayed at the camp and had school.

Connecting the Dots . . .

We live in an extremely "me" oriented culture. People of European nations look at our movies, Internet sites, and blogs and make jokes about the self-centered Americans. We are often depicted as "haughty, self-absorbed, and self-indulgent consumers."

The British people warn us: "Wake up, cousins. Look what has happened to our country. Please don't follow our footsteps. You deserve better."

Do we deserve better? We are a nation stuck on ourselves, often heady with our perceived prosperity. We need a good dose of humility. If you ever travel to another continent or third-world country, you'll be surprised at how helpless we really are without all our conveniences.

We think we are so safe because the fighting we hear about is always "over there." Realize that the real threat is not from somewhere else but from within. It is from our own lack of commitment to upholding the morals and freedoms our forefathers passed on to us. Our generation had freedom and prosperity served to us on a fine china platter, and look what we've done with it. We've set it on the garbage bin, where it balances precariously and is about to fall in and shatter.

Consider what it would be like to really lose everything—your home, your livelihood, your country. Now do something with those sobering thoughts.

Think about it.

CHAPTER 18

Never Forgotten

While my twin and I had been traveling with the youth in trains, our family had been on the move also. My sister and I heard news that our family had left our home and had crossed the border out of Yugoslavia. We did not know exactly where they were.

One Sunday morning, I woke up very early—around five or five thirty. We were sleeping upstairs in the dentist's house. The bedroom was not heated. This was winter in Czechoslovakia, and it was very cold. In order to keep warm, each night we would warm the bed with heated bricks wrapped in cloth. Then we'd dig ourselves under a large, down-filled comforter.

This particular morning, I heard a voice downstairs that sounded like my dad. I quickly shook my sister and said, "I think Dad's here!"

She peeked her head out from under the comforter and said, "What makes you think so?"

I told her that I thought I heard him clear his throat. He had this way of clearing his throat when he was nervous.

She replied with disbelief, *"Ach, du bist ja verücht!"* ("You have gone crazy!") She continued, "You want to see Dad so much that now you're even hearing his voice!" Then she covered her head back up.

I said, "Well, fine, but I'm going down." I got out of bed and began getting dressed.

My twin then scrambled out of bed and said, "Wait for me." We got dressed and ran downstairs.

Sure enough, there was Dad! What a joy. We hugged him and cried, thinking, *Yippee, now we can go with Dad.*

Dad had been traveling for days and looked so different from when we had last seen him. His clothes were all rumpled, and his beard had been growing for three days. We had never seen him look so unkempt. But we didn't care; we were so overjoyed to see him. We told him that we would go pack our bags and leave with him.

He said, "*Oh nein, Kinder.* You two can't come with me now. I will get you someday. I will send you letters. In the letters, I will let you know when I will come get you and when we will leave this area. Read them carefully, and pay special attention to them. That is very important. Very important," he emphasized.

I'm glad he emphasized this because my emotions were on a roller coaster—just being glad to see him, then his condition, then thinking we'd be able to go with him, and now having been told to wait longer. I'm glad he made me pay attention.

The reason he was able to find us was that he had become an assistant to the refugee camp manager where they were staying in Görlitz, Germany. Görlitz was not very far from where we were living with the dentist and his family in Czechoslovakia. As assistant to the camp manager, Dad traveled around the area to find the best buys for rations for their camp. In each village that he visited, he asked people if they knew where the girl refugees had been taken. While inquiring at one town, a lady told him that she had been to Neustadt an der Tofelfichte and seen two redheaded twins. Twins were rare, especially redheaded twins, so that was how Dad knew where to search. He went to the girls' camp leader and asked where we had been placed. She told him that we were with the dentist's family.

The week after Dad's visit, my twin had a severe asthma attack. She was rushed to Prague, Czechoslovakia. Dad was allowed to take her home with him to live at their refugee camp in Görlitz, Germany, but I had to stay with the Hitler Youth in Neustadt an der Tofelfichte in Czechoslovakia. That was the hardest thing to do, to say "good-bye" to my twin. Now I was all alone. I was the youngest of eight children, and I had always had some member of my family with me. And now I had no one. My family had each other in the camp, but I truly felt as if I were abandoned, all alone. Yes, I had Jesus, so I was not really all alone, but I was twelve years old, and this was hard.

When Dad came to get my twin's clothing, he again gave me strict orders to read the mail carefully. Letters were censored, so he had to be very discreet when he told me anything in them. He would choose to encode certain words in the Hungarian language interspersed amongst the German. I loved the Hungarian language. In fact, there was a time I could communicate better in Hungarian than in German. The Hungarian language is more sweet and tender, with a beautiful cadence, in contrast to the German language, which tends to be more harsh and throaty. I preferred the softer impression of the Hungarian tongue.

I stayed with the dentist and his wife in Neustadt an der Tofelfichte for three or four weeks, until the government had obtained housing for us refugee children. The government did this by conscripting homes or large buildings and equipping them for lodging or for school. I was moved to a big house that was not too far from the girls' refugee camp. This house was large enough to accommodate all of the girls who had been in private homes. It really had been much better living in a private home.

There were about twenty of us girls sleeping in a huge room filled with bunk beds. The building was so cold that we had six military blankets on each bunk bed. Six blankets were very difficult to fold in order to meet the regulation requirements of our supervisors. The beds had to be made military style, with the corners and sides tucked so smoothly that a coin could bounce off of them. We had to be certain every item was in its proper place and that the room appeared picture perfect to pass inspection. Then we would head to the camp for breakfast and continue the rest of our school day.

If our bed did not pass inspection, when we returned to the house, it would be a mess. The bed would be totally torn apart. And we would receive demerits for our lack of perfection. We girls learned to work together to help each other so we would all pass inspection. It's a good thing my dad had taught us about the need for orderliness at home. He really did know what he was doing when he was preparing me.

While I was there, my dad, still in Görlitz, Germany, wrote me letters in German. He would also encode some Hungarian words. It was through these letters that I learned that I needed to meet my older sister at the courthouse in Neustadt an der Tofelfichte on a specified day, at a specific time.

The problem was that I did not have a permit to leave my girls' refugee camp in Neustadt an der Tofelfichte. I had to sneak out. Thankfully, my sleeping quarters were away from the girls' camp and in the big house, so I was able to take my clothing without being seen by someone in the camp. I did tell one girl that I was leaving, but she promised to keep my secret until I was gone. As far as I know, she kept her word to me.

I was afraid that the camp leaders would search for me, thinking they had lost a child. But my dad had assured me that a letter was on the way, which gave permission for me to leave to be with my family. That letter of permission would not arrive until after I needed to leave. I was still twelve when I had to disobey the rules of the camp to go meet my sister.

I sneaked out of the house and went to the courthouse. The weather was freezing cold, with blowing snow. The ground was already covered with snow. I carefully hurried along and found my way to the courthouse. I tried to avoid looking at people's faces so as not to be recognized by anyone. After all, I was supposed to be in school classes.

I finally arrived, half frozen; my skin was chafed and my fingers nearly numb. I stood shivering at the entrance, waiting for my sister. Soon I was so cold that I couldn't stand still any longer. I started to cry. So I started walking, circling the courthouse, waiting for my sister.

Little did I know that my sister, who was also freezing cold, was doing the same thing. We were both walking around the outside of the courthouse and feeling more anxious with each passing minute. This walking in the blizzard, circling the courthouse, seemed to go on forever. My sister was behind me the entire time, but since my head was covered and I was all bundled up and coated with a layer of snow and ice, she did not recognize me from behind. She was the smart one. She turned around and went the opposite direction. We bumped right into each other. We hugged, and we cried.

We prayed and ran to the train station. We held hands to help each other. All the way, the "what ifs" of fear were racing through our minds. We were two young girls in a strange city with no money, just train tickets. We did not have permission from the authorities to be out by ourselves. We could both be in big trouble if we were found out. Where would we stay if we could not make the train? And what would our family do? What would Dad say? "Oh, God, please help us!"

The multi-track train station was busy with incoming soldiers, outgoing refugees, and local people. Just as we arrived, the voice on the loud speaker notified us that the train Dad was expecting us to be on was pulling out of the station. We were too late! We had wasted too much time circling around the courthouse and had missed our train. We cried, and we kept praying.

As we were leaving the gate of the train platform, we met the cook from my camp. She asked what I was doing there. I told her that we were trying to get to my family but we had missed our train. As we were talking to her, the loud speaker announced that a special train, *a Sonderzug*, was leaving for Görlitz. This type of train was a special chartered train and granted priority privileges on the tracks to reach its destination in a shorter amount of time. This train had brought soldiers in and was taking refugees out. What a joy and what relief. Praise God! He is never late, even when we are. He is always on time.

Our train arrived in Görlitz before the train that we were supposed to be on arrived. Our parents never knew the difference. We were so excited. We hugged and thanked God! I was so grateful that I had not been forgotten. I was not alone. I was back with my family.

Dad picked us up at the station and took us to the refugee camp, where the rest of the family was staying. We were reunited with Mom, my youngest brother, my twin, and my Aunt Barbara. The following day, we were planning to take the train from Görlitz to Dresden. Our goal was to travel to Austria, where my brother Konrad was stationed. At the time, it was more peaceful in Austria. Many other people were hoping to get to Switzerland, which was a neutral country and also more peaceful. It was legal for us to travel, but the camp manager did not want the other refugees to know our plans. He was afraid everyone else would want to leave.

It was already dark outside when we arrived at the camp. The inside had very large rooms, as if it had been a hotel with banquet rooms at one time. The room we slept in housed forty people, sleeping three people on each of its high bunk beds. We were planning to leave secretly the next morning, even leaving some of our possessions behind and hoping that no one would realize that we had left until later that evening.

The next morning, as we were preparing to leave, chaos broke out in the camp. Rumors that the war was moving closer had caused everyone to panic. Since my dad was the assistant manager, he was unable to leave. My dad went about his work but wanted us to stay in the room together since things were so chaotic outside. After going through so much to finally get most of his family together, he did not want anything more to happen to us. So we did not leave the camp until three days later than we had initially planned.

Three days later, we went to the train station, but there was not enough room on the train for us. My brother and older sister were able to squeeze into the train. My brother had crawled through a window. At that time, people would pack into trains like sardines in a can. The trains were standing room only. It was so crowded that people were hanging onto the outside of the train, and some of the people inside even passed out. It was an awful time, with everyone wanting to leave and get to a safer place.

We didn't know it at the time, but the end of the war was near. This was February of 1945, and the war ended in May of 1945. Things were very chaotic and tense. Dad told my brother and sister to get off because he wanted all seven of us to stay together. My siblings got off the train, and the train left without us.

As the train pulled away, we saw a family of nine across the tracks from us. They were from the same refugee camp and hadn't made the train either.

I asked my dad, "What are we going to do?"

He replied, "We just pray, and God will show us the way."

In less than an hour, a special train arrived that was not scheduled to run that day, and they allowed us and the other family to get on since there had been no room on the first train. Only two families traveled on that train. God is faithful!

Connecting the Dots . . .

Do you make connecting God's dots a habit? It is important to make it a habit so that you can help your children look for the silver lining in all things. Train them to find the good, to look for it like a prospector searching for gold. If you look for it, you will find it, and your treasure store of faith will be vastly enriched. Have fun connecting God's dots in your life!

The Bible says, "Can a mother forget the baby at her breast and have no compassion on the child she has borne? Though she may forget, I will not forget you! See, I have engraved you on the palms of my hands" (Isaiah 49:15–16).

Think about it.

CHAPTER 19

A Miracle of God's Perfect Protection

Little did I know that if we had left the refugee camp on the day we had planned, I would not be alive today to tell this story. As we were arriving at Dresden, we saw smoke and broken, uprooted tracks. Many homes and much of the station were destroyed. We found out that the Royal Air Force (RAF) and the United States Air Force (USAF) had bombed that vicinity three days prior, using incendiary bombs. Estimates vary, but tens of thousands of people had died.

There were a number of refugees who, fleeing westward from the advancing Russian forces, were in Dresden at the time of the bombings. This number of refugees, which is estimated from train arrivals, foot traffic, and emergency accommodations, places the number of refugees between 100,000 and 200,000. The people who were killed were old people, women, children, and fleeing refugees. Many of those people were trying to get out of Dresden to safer places. There had been little or no military stationed there.

The scene was horrific, assaulting all our senses. I have never smelled so much burned hair and so many burned bones in my life. I will never forget this. People were looting the dead bodies for gold teeth, rings, jewelry, and other valuables before loading them onto trucks to take them to large graves outside of the city. I pray that no one will ever have to experience what we saw there. This was especially difficult because of my young age. It will be imbedded in my mind forever.

People were crying and saying "good-bye" to family members and lovers. Little children were wandering around, crying out for care. Every few hours, a person with loudspeakers would come walking around, calling out the name of a lost individual.

Our family took all of this in as we stayed on the platform of the train station that had been partially cleared of debris. We hid ourselves among the rubble and remains of what had been the station platform. We stayed there for about forty-eight hours. It was cold, so we slept sitting next to each other, trying to stay warm.

While we were there, there were two more air raids. There were bomb shelters available, but the shelters were overflowing. If too many people were in the shelters, the people inside would suffocate. There were also underground bomb shelters in the basements of the buildings in the business district. But our father told us we must not go into those underground shelters because of the hot and cold water lines that ran just above them. In Europe, then and now, many areas of cities are supplied with hot water from a central heating plant. The pipes that run through the city from that heating plant can be several feet in diameter. If a bomb hit a hot water pipe and it burst, the people below would be scalded, drowned, or worse. So our family stayed on the rubble-filled platform, covered up with luggage and coats and blankets so that the pilots in the airplanes would not be able to tell that there were people there. Thankfully, no more bombs were dropped.

The Red Cross was such a blessing during this time. They had arrived, bringing small sandwiches, doughnut holes, soup, and coffee. They even had hot chocolate for the children. They worked around the clock, caring for people.

Finally, we left and went to Schwarzach, Austria. From there, we went to Zell am See, where Konrad picked us up. He was stationed in Aufhausen and had some friends who had a room for us to stay in, but only for a short time. The family's last name was Arnold.

We searched for housing, but it was extremely difficult to secure. In March, we moved out of the Arnolds' household and into a chicken coop. The chickens had just been taken out. It was a huge, filthy building. We whitewashed the inside and scrubbed the floors with lye. However, despite the thorough cleaning, all of us contracted head lice.

Since the building was too large to heat, we tied up ropes and hung blankets from them to make a smaller room, in which we lived. We heated this room by using a small stove. To keep ourselves off the cold floor, we built trough-like beds out of two by fours. We filled them with blankets and covered ourselves up with down-filled comforters. We only built two large beds, so four people could sleep on each bed. Living in these conditions was not good for our well-being. We contracted many colds and were often sick.

Since we were still required to go to school, we needed to get rid of the lice. To do this, we put gasoline on our heads and wrapped them with cloths. We kept those on for an entire night. It was so smelly and horrible, not to mention that it burned a lot. We wanted to get the caps off, but we had to rid ourselves of the lice.

Once we could take the caps off, we needed to wash our hair. But with limited ration cards, it was difficult for us to get our hair smelling better for school. The gasoline had just soaked in. It was such a mess.

We lived in the chicken coop for about six weeks, until Herr Islitzer found us two rooms in a farmhouse that already had three other families living there. This farmhouse was in Fürth Kaprun and was owned by Herr Aberger. There we had a kitchen, in which we kept one bed and a cot, a little table with a bench, three chairs, seven or eight plates, a few cups, a few glasses, a few pots and pans, a few pieces of silverware we had brought from home, and a stove. We had no kitchen sink, no running water, one light bulb per room, and one outhouse for all of the renters. We slept four people in the kitchen, three people on a twin-sized bed, and one person on the cot. My parents' room had two beds. They slept in one, and my brother was in the other.

It is amazing how we went from riches to rags in such a short span of time. However, we were so grateful for what we did have. Like the apostle Paul, we "learned, in whatsoever state I am, therewith to be content" (Philippians 4:11 KJV).

While living in these two rooms of Herr Aberger's farmhouse in Fürth, we set about to obtain employment and complete our education. My father obtained employment with a building contractor. My older sister, who was sixteen years old, got a position working in the household of the owners of a noodle factory. My brother, who was fifteen years old, was able to get a mechanic's apprenticeship. All of these positions were in Zell am See, which was several kilometers from Fürth. Initially, the working members of the family took the train each day, and then, later on, they purchased bicycles.

My twin and I, still twelve-year-olds, attended school in Piesendorf, which was about a forty-five minute walk one way. This was very hard for my twin with her asthma, especially during the snowy weather. I used to walk ahead of her, carrying her books and making a path for her, all the while praying, "*Himmel Vater*, so much air, yet so hard for Sis to take it in. *Bitte*, help her to make the walk." And He always did.

School was done by late afternoon, and we walked home. Then I would go to a forest near our house and gather firewood. We did not have a permit to fell trees as the local people did, but we did get a permit to gather limbs from the forest floor. We burned the limbs in the kitchen stove. This provided heat for our two rooms; a way to cook; and heated water for bathing, washing, cooking, cleaning, etc. It was not easy, but we felt God's presence with us.

We got ration tickets, which were issued at the courthouse and were valid for a one-month period. There were three types of tickets: infant, youth and adult. The ration tickets gave us permission to purchase designated items when the specific number or letter on our tickets was published in the newspaper along with the date that letter or number would be available. Each letter or number on the ticket would be linked to a specific item such as: flour, bread, milk, butter, meat or "special" and the quantity of that item that the bearer of the ticket would be permitted to purchase. I spent many hours each week waiting in line to purchase items at the baker's, butcher's, and grocer's businesses. Many times, when I finally reached the front of the line, the item was all gone, and rarely was a "rain check" issued.

Life was not easy. Since there were shortages of everything, most of the national people were not willing to share, especially with refugees who had little with which to barter and who seemed to be competing for these already limited resources. Many days we ate just cornbread and skimmed milk and potatoes. This was the pattern, especially near the end of the month, as our supplies were depleted. But we still considered ourselves blessed.

Through all of this, "necessity was the mother of invention." My mother was amazing. She continued to create things out of "nothing," or so it seemed. On the weekends, I worked for our landlord, a farmer, as well as Herr Islitzer. I helped clean their houses, wash clothes, and harvest hay. In return, they would give us some eggs, milk, and butter. One day, Herr Islitzer gave me some soybeans. I brought them home, and Mom said, with a little sparkle in her eye, "Ohhhhh." I soon forgot all about it.

One day that same week, when we all got home from work and school, we smelled *"Nuss Streudel"* (nut strudel). We looked at each other questioningly. Mom had made vegetable soup and had nut strudel for dessert. My dad asked, "Where did you get nuts for strudel?" She said she would never tell. She did not want him to know that they were really soybeans and not nuts.

We had no intention of permanently staying in Austria. Shortly after we arrived, we had begun the process of applying for visas to immigrate to the United States of America. A sponsor in the United States was needed for us to be allowed to apply for visas. We knew several families that, years earlier, had emigrated from Crvenka. These families were willing to sponsor us. They had settled in northern Indiana. We thought this would be a fairly quick process, and that in itself gave us hope. We thought that we would soon be in the USA and able to start again in earnest. Little did we know that the approval for our visas would take six long years.

We had come to Austria because my second eldest brother, Konrad, was stationed there. As the end of the war came closer, his regiment was moved to Germany, where he was captured and placed in an American prisoner-of-war camp. Initially, Konrad had been included on our visa application. However, two years into the application process, he died. He had contracted tuberculosis.

War is war. The realities are unconscionable. Rations had been issued for the prisoners. Unfortunately, the rations never reached the prisoners because much of the food was sold on the black market. So the prisoners were starving. The United States Government became aware of the starvation in their own prison camp because the building construction projects were not progressing as quickly as they had anticipated. German prisoners were the manual labor for these construction projects, and most prisoners at this camp were too sick to work with any vigor. This lack of productivity prompted an investigation. The investigation revealed that the prisoners had only been provided soup made from potato peels, grass and water.

Those in higher authority immediately opened the "floodgates of food" to the starving prisoners, in an attempt to restore their health. However, by this time, the health of most of the prisoners was far too damaged, and my brother was one of them. My parents obtained a visa from the Americans to visit Konrad in a hospital in Germany. He was able to relate this information to my parents six weeks before he died. Konrad's death required that we change our visa to the United States and reapply. So we continued to work, wait, and pray.

Although the Austrians in the area in which we were living spoke German (Deutsch), their dialect was very different from our German dialect. Our dialect from Crvenka would have been called a *"Schwäbische"* dialect of German. All of our family also knew *Hoch Deutsch*, or High German, as well as Hungarian, and Slavish. We had a very difficult time communicating with this different Austrian regional dialect of German. We could get by if they could also speak High German, but otherwise, it was very frustrating. It took us children about four months to master the new dialect. My parents and aunt never did master it. It was a constant reminder that we were foreigners.

Connecting the Dots . . .

There is a map in this book that shows the dots of my journey in Europe. Each of those dots holds special meaning. They are proof, yet again, of God's faithfulness.

Maps are great. They let us know where we are and where we've been, and they present us with various options for where we'd like to go. Maps were a great idea.

Do you have a record of your life's journey? Consider leaving such a legacy to your children. It could be the map that helps guide them in the future.

Think about it.

CHAPTER 20

The Sun Begins to Shine Again

Everyone's attitude improved immensely when the war ended in May of 1945. A tremendous pressure was released, and now we refugees could even be acknowledged as people with feelings, needs, and value. People were much more friendly and willing to share. For me, being so relational, this was like a ray of sunshine breaking through after a long, cold darkness.

The house we lived in was located in Fürth. Fürth was a very small village. It had two big farms, a few small ones, a train stop, a horse farrier, and a small beer room. Its main recognition was being the turning point to the town of Kaprun, which had the *Stauwerk*. The Kaprun Stauwerk is a huge hydroelectric plant that is primarily supplied by the meltwater from the Pasterze Glacier on the Grossglockner Mountain that collects into the Margaritze and Mooserboden Reservoirs. This hydroelectric plant was built inside the mountain, utilizing the labors of many individuals who had come from occupied territories during World War II. In 2012, the Kaprun Stauwerk completed another upgrade, which more than doubled its capacity, making it one of the largest producers of hydroelectric power in Austria and Europe.

The town of Kaprun had an old castle called "Schloss Kaprun." When we were living in Kaprun, the castle's most recent use was as a storage site for spoils from the war. Word got out that the military was going to open the doors of the castle to the public for one day. This opening was in order to allow the people to freely take any items they could use. It was going to be on a first-come, first-served basis. So I got there early, and the place was packed. People were pushing and shoving. Everyone needed something.

I was fortunate to get two large bolts of fabric. We needed fabric. The fabric was checkered blue and white. One bolt was heavy weight; the other was lighter weight. The fabric was originally used to make uniforms for prisoners of war. I also got a pair of shoes. I wanted to get something for my dad, but all I could find was a cigar clipper. It was silver and in the shape of a dog's head. My dad did not smoke cigars, but it's the thought that counts.

My mom used the blue-and-white checkered cloth to make everything. She made curtains, sheets, tablecloths, dish towels, shirts, dirndls, aprons, and even underwear. The cloth was a godsend. It became our identifying trademark. The house we were sharing had an upstairs level with a balcony and a clothesline. So, when the weather permitted, we would hang our blue-and-white checkered clothes from the line. All the passersby would chuckle, "Frau Welker has done her laundry today." The clothing looked pretty good, and we were thankful because we certainly did not have enough money to purchase cloth or other items from the market.

Piesendorf, the town where we attended school, was also where we attended worship services. The only church available was a Catholic church, so that is where we went. We also received Catholic catechism each week in our school. The school in Piesendorf taught students up through fifteen years of age. Very few of the residents in that town had much higher education than that.

I completed all the schooling available in Piesendorf, but we did not have funds for me to attend a university. So I needed to obtain full-time employment. My father got a full-time job for me at the noodle factory when I was not quite fifteen years of age. This was not my first job, by any means, but the others had just been part-time jobs.

Dad had always impressed on me, "Whatever job you get, Hilda, you stick it out, because you need to have a job." And I did. As I look back, I think the reason he was so adamant about my having a job was that he saw so many young women getting into trouble. By this time, the area was filled with many children born out of wedlock.

My job at the noodle factory was to take the noodles to the drying room. A worker at the top level would put dough through the extruder, which would form the noodles at the bottom. I placed a rod at this lower position to catch the bundle of noodles. I then cut the noodles and ran the rod with the noodles draped over it to the drying room. Before leaving on my run, I had to set an empty rod in position to catch the next batch. I had to move quickly in order to return in time to catch the new batch. If I did not, the noodles would become a ball of dough again. If this happened, the worker feeding the dough would become angry. Unfortunately, along the way, there were many men who would make comments and try to ask me for a date. I wasn't interested in that. I had to get back to catch my noodles.

The noodle factory was not for me. The task itself was okay, but the environment was completely opposite of my Christian upbringing. And it did not live up to my expectations of the Austrian people. The emotional pressures of the previous decade were shockingly obvious in the illicit behaviors that were openly displayed there. Many people had lost everything—their loved ones, their finances, their hopes and dreams. They too had gone through war. And, as a byproduct, alcoholism and prostitution were very commonplace. The whole experience was very frightening to me, so I prayed a lot.

One day my father asked me how I liked it. He had no idea what it was like working on the noodle factory floor.

I sadly told him, "Dad, if this is what life is all about, I don't want any part of it."

Dad was surprised and said, "Oh, really? Well, for now, just make the best of it. Maybe our visas will come soon."

I did not tell him about the harassment. I knew he had enough to worry about. I continued to pray desperately that I could find another job.

Connecting the Dots . . .

The harassment that I faced is altogether too prevalent in our schools and workplaces today. Help your children to realize that if an event, conversation, or social setting makes them feel uncomfortable, they should not participate in it. Counsel your children about how they should respond in situations like that.

Dialog with your children to design a plan, an exit strategy that they will own, that will help them to disengage from these situations. Work with your children to develop a script for common scenarios that will teach them how they might verbally and physically respond. Practice those scripts so that your children can be ready to thoughtfully respond if the need presents itself. Pray for your children, their peers, and their generation.

Think about it.

CHAPTER 21

No More Noodles!

God answered my prayer. Since I did most of the food purchasing for our family, I got to know the owners of the businesses pretty well. The owner of the grocery store was related to the dentist of Piesendorf. The dentist, Dr. Dittenberger, was looking for a dental apprentice. The grocer recommended me to Dr. Dittenberger and told me to go apply for the position. Since I was not quite fifteen years old, he asked me to bring my father with me for the first interview.

During this initial interview with my father, Dr. Dittenberger described the basics of my required hygiene, uniforms, and in-office demeanor. He had several other applicants and said that he should be completed with his interviews by Monday of the next week. I quit the noodle factory on Friday and returned to Dr. Dittenberger's office on Monday for the final interview.

During that final interview, Dr. Dittenberger detailed to me the requirements of my apprenticeship, should I be selected. He described how especially difficult the first three months of the apprenticeship would be for me. He said that after those first three months, he would be able to accurately determine if I would be able to complete the dental apprenticeship. The Doctor of Dentistry apprenticeship in Austria was for three years. It required additional years of apprenticeship to complete the Surgeon of Dentistry degree.

I did get the opportunity to learn the profession of dentistry from Dr. Dittenberger. I was praising God—so many miracles. Dr. Dittenberger knew we were refugees and had applied for visas; yet, over all the local applicants, God had him choose me for this wonderful opportunity, which appeared all the more radiant in comparison to the noodle factory. I made an oath to myself there and then that I would do whatever was required, above and beyond, to be successful in this godsend of a position.

We did not have any uniforms, so Mrs. Dittenberger, Gabriella, gave me a uniform of hers that I was able to take home for my mom to use as a pattern to make additional uniforms for me. Dr. Dittenberger also gave me two dentistry textbooks to study and memorize—one for the operating room, the other for the lab.

Little did the Dittenbergers realize that we had no material for uniforms, so we used white bedding sheets. Nor did we own a sewing machine. So Herr Islitzer found us an old sewing machine, and Mom made me both the uniform lab coats and some skirts. The skirts she made out of blankets.

It was a good thing that I had worked at the noodle factory, and I thank God that I had made that oath of determination to stick it out. Dr. Dittenberger had told the honest truth. Those first three months of apprenticeship, since I was now on my own, were the hardest trial of my young life. Many days, I was tempted to quit. I needed to walk to work by 6 A.M. because our first patient arrived at 7 A.M. And I had to have everything in order for the day. Initially, I walked to work, but later, Dr. Dittenberger gave me his wife's bicycle. On the way home, I would try to envision what my dad would say if I quit Dr. Dittenberger's apprenticeship. Then I would remember the noodle factory. By the time I arrived home, I had resolved that I had better stick it out at Dr. Dittenberger's.

I had to sterilize the instruments and pay vigilant attention to every word the doctor said and every look he gave. I had to hand him the exact instruments out of a vast array of choices. And I had to do this without causing a pause in his work as I was trying to recall all the new terminology I had been memorizing from my dental texts. I had to learn how to mix impression material for making dentures, crowns, inlays, and bridges. I also had to learn how to pour the material into the models and complete the processes to make these dental appliances. I actually became very practiced in this dental lab work, which would serve me well in the future.

We examined patients from 7:00 in the morning until noon. If we were on time, we had some lunch. But I usually did not have any lunch because I had eaten it on my way to work. So, while Dr. and Mrs. Dittenberger were having lunch, I would stay in the office, clean up, and prepare for the afternoon appointments.

We saw patients all afternoon, worked emergencies in, and were usually completed by about 5:30–6:00 P.M. Then I would clean up the instruments and prepare for the next day's work schedule. In the winter, when it got dark earlier, Mrs. Dittenberger would make certain I got out in time to make it home with some light.

The dental practice was on the ground floor of the Dittenberger's home. They lived upstairs. One day I saved my lunch to eat it during the lunch break. For some reason, Dr. Dittenberger came down to the office as I was unwrapping my lunch. He was shocked when he saw that my lunch was just a small piece of bread with butter. He said, "Is that all you have to eat for lunch?"

I said, "Yes, Doctor."

He pointed with his arm to the stairs leading to their living quarters and said, "You get upstairs. From now on, you are eating with us!"

That was another blessing from God. That day, I went home thanking God again for His bountiful provision, knowing what a wonderful gift this would be for my mom. Now she would be able to save more food for my growing brother, who was seventeen.

I walked into the house and told Mom, "You don't have to fix a lunch for me anymore."

She replied, "What are you talking about? You must eat."

Then I told her the wonderful news, and we shared joyful tears of thanks.

After the first six weeks, things got better, and I was no longer tempted to quit. Besides, I had made that oath. As I continued to gain competence, I began to feel at home in the profession and bonded with the Dittenberger family.

One day Dr. Dittenberger told me to clear the appointment schedule for an upcoming afternoon. He said there was a special event he and Mrs. Dittenberger were going to attend that afternoon. So I cleared the schedule as he instructed me.

That day arrived, and after our morning patient exams were completed, I cleaned up as usual, as if the day were done.

Then we went upstairs to the kitchen, where we normally ate lunch, but the kitchen table was empty. Dr. Dittenberger opened the doors to the formal dining room and said, "Today we are eating in here."

Oh my! The table was loaded with special foods, and there were four guests already seated at the table. Usually the doctor's wife, Gabriella, sat at his right side, so I moved to sit in an empty seat. He said, "Oh no. From this day forward, you are my right hand, so you sit here at my right side." Then everyone sat down, and we had a toast. It had been three months, and I had made it. Thank You, Jesus!

Now I understood why my dad had been so intentional about training me to think and to work. He taught me not to merely get by but also to exceed expectations. I was to do everything as if I were doing it for God. Dad was successful in his mission. Despite all the chaos and pressures of war, we were able to survive and to thrive with our virtues intact.

Connecting the Dots . . .

All of that intentional parenting does pay off when a child succeeds, when he or she has developed the character that can run the race and stick it out. When your children can keep to the course despite valleys, mountains, and rock-strewn paths, they have developed perseverance.

Perseverance is likely the single most important virtue that successful people possess. It will get your child farther than being smart, beautiful, or witty. With perseverance, your child can fly, or at least, he or she can find the next best option.

By developing perseverance, your children can legitimately develop competence. Practice makes permanent, and practicing the desired techniques of most any discipline will develop competence. Once your children have gained competence, they also can become confident—at least in one specific arena. There are always more arenas, but with competence and confidence, each child has developed the pattern with which he or she can succeed. The mold is cast, and now your child can apply this to nearly all aspects of life. Your child has arrived. It's time to celebrate.

Think about it.

CHAPTER 22

Oops! We lost our patient

I was back to work as usual. Each day I was gaining new insights into the profession and getting more into the routine. I found that I really loved dentistry, but more than that, I loved the people.

One day I was mixing some alloy when I felt a sharp pain in my right abdominal area. I quickly set the bowl down and grasped the chair to prevent myself from falling. Immediately, Dr. Dittenberger realized that I was having an appendix attack. He called the physician, Doctor Gratzer, who immediately sent me by train to the hospital in Zell am See. They also called my father, who met me at the hospital.

The hospital was overflowing with patients. They had no available rooms and only a cot unoccupied. So I got the cot. The doctor said, "Appendix. Put her in the operating room."

The nurse put me in the operating room, turned off the light, closed the door, and left. I fell asleep and woke up in the middle of the night, holding my side. I finally realized where I was and wondered where everyone else was.

They found me the next morning and realized that they had forgotten me the night before. My father had seen them put me on the cot, and they had told him they would take care of me and that he should return in the morning. When he returned the next morning, I was in surgery.

What a mess. My appendix had burst. The doctors worked on me for six hours, trying to clean the infected material from my abdominal cavity. Then they put drainage tubes in. I was in the hospital for six weeks with those drainage tubes and then was sent home with drainage tubes. I even had to return to work with those drainage tubes. Yuck! The doctors said it was a miracle that I pulled through. I knew that it was God who pulled me through. He still had more for me to do.

As my dental apprenticeship with Dr. Dittenberger continued, I gained firsthand experience in working with socialized medicine. While it may sound appealing to have a guaranteed insurance plan that is managed through the government, in reality, it was not a good thing. Rather, it was a nightmare. Oh, sure, we had plenty of patients, and our schedule was always full, but the government did not reimburse the doctors very well. And since those on government insurance did not feel they personally were paying for our services, it was not unusual for them to forget their appointments. So we learned to double book the schedules. If a patient came in offering cash, we booked them immediately for the same day. Cash-paying clients always took precedence over government patients, unless it was an emergency.

Shortly after my appendix episode, our family was notified by the United States Department of Immigration that it was time for us to have our physical exams. These physical examinations were conducted at a specific facility in Salzburg. It was a huge facility with hundreds of immigrants getting physical exams. These exams were not conducted in private; although, men and women were examined separately.

We all had to disrobe and do as ordered: "Open your mouth, spread your legs, bend over . . ." as they checked every orifice of our bodies—one examiner on our front side, the other at our back side. How embarrassing! I felt so humiliated and embarrassed for myself and my family. I had never seen my own mother disrobed before. We just tried to look at the floor and cover ourselves with our hands as best as we could. What an experience! I hope I never have to experience that again.

Connecting the Dots . . .

Welcome to socialized medicine. There are too many patients, too few resources, and no incentive for excellence in care. In socialized medicine, the providers work like mice on a treadmill, going round and round. While pushed to meet efficiency quotas, the healthcare providers in socialized medicine have no margin to mete out the main component of the healing arts—relationship. There is no time to truly care for the patients, no time to listen, no time to counsel. Practitioners in socialized medicine spend more time documenting than in actual patient contact. Is that the kind of profession bright minds will choose to enter? I don't think so.

If you are a patient, whom do you want performing your surgery? The surgeon who has the most experience and highest rate of success, or whoever is on your socialized medicine health plan?

"Oh, and by the way, you'll need to take a number. Our next available appointment is twelve months out. How old will you be by then? Oh, you may not qualify. We take the younger patients first. Sorry. Keep checking back; maybe something will open up . . . Next!"

"Oh (silence) . . . you have a special-needs child? Well, your family has met their healthcare allotment . . . forever. Really throws our efficiency metrics off. Sorry. We only have limited resources. Don't call back . . . Next!"

Or maybe you are in the healing professions; perhaps you are a dedicated healthcare provider struggling with how you will respond when asked to perform an abortion. Maybe you are a healthcare professional burnt out with the sheer number of government regulations mandating your abilities to care for your patients. You are giving serious thoughts to a career change. You'd retire completely, but junior is still in high school.

Perhaps you're a compassionate student whose dreams have been dashed by the edicts of a new socialist reform. Or maybe you are a faithful pastor denied access to provide spiritual comfort and prayer to your parishioner in the hospital. You are thinking about it and you are praying about it. Let us pray that all Americans will consider the implications of socialized medicine, and choose thoughtfully to maintain our religious and moral freedoms. Freedoms that have enabled the medical community of the United States to attract the gifted, dedicated practitioners that have earned it the reputation of excellence in the healing arts.

Think about it.

CHAPTER 23

Waiting and Watching

Life went on as usual. The mailman knew we were waiting for our visas, and when he came, he'd shake his head "no."

Mom had been sick. We didn't really know what was wrong, but she could not keep food down. The doctor recommended that my father take mom to the hospital in Schwarzach. So he did. Mom stayed in the Schwarzach hospital for at least six weeks, where they diagnosed that she had a thyroid-gland infection and possibly cancer of the thyroid. But my father did not permit the doctors to do surgery. He was concerned that if it was cancerous, surgery would cause it to spread.

It had been my habit since beginning my apprenticeship to pray at each kilometer marker on my walk or ride to work. I would pray for my yet-missing family members—my eldest sister and my brother Eduard—and now I added praying for my mom to get well. I reasoned with God that Mom must get well because my father could get another wife but I would never get another mother.

Again, God answered my prayers. One day my eldest sister and her husband showed up. They had found us through church friends in Salzburg. Shortly after their arrival, my brother Eduard showed up. He had located us through Salzburg friends.

Mom did not improve in the hospital, and the doctors gave up hope. So Dad and my brother Eduard went to bring her home from the hospital at Schwarzach, thinking that if she were going to die soon, it would be better for her to be surrounded by her loving family. She was very, very ill when she got back home.

We contacted a doctor friend we had met who was also a refugee. Dad had known him as a surgeon in the military. This doctor was now working as a nurse at the nearby clinic for the workers at the Stauwerk. He came to the house and confirmed that mom's health situation was indeed very bad. He had a small amount of medication to give her. This was to help her keep her food down. He cautioned us that this was all the medication he could obtain. But if, perhaps, by some miracle, it could help mom keep food down, she might improve.

And it did help. But she had lost so much blood that she was anemic and needed blood. None of the blood banks carried her blood type. Thank God again, my sister's blood type matched Mom's, and that helped to save her life. This same doctor friend performed the blood transfusion for my mom at the clinic in which he worked after regular business hours.

So God answered our prayers, and I had my mom for twenty-seven more years! She even visited the nurses at the Schwarzach hospital. They exclaimed, "Is it you or your ghost?" They were so amazed that she was alive and healthy.

Since mom was still recuperating, my older sister quit her job to stay at home and help mom with all the household chores. My sister also began taking correspondence courses to complete her professional teaching license.

We knew that we would need coats for our immigration to the United States. All of us needed coats. But we could not afford to purchase them or even afford the material to make them. Eventually, my dad found some beige yarn. For some reason, the people did not like the color or quality, so he got it at a very reasonable cost to us. Then he found a large weaving unit. He set up the unit in the kitchen, where we girls slept. My older sister then spent her days using the beige yarn to weave fabric for our coats. She did an amazing job of weaving this precious fabric. After it was finished, my dad took the fabric to the local tailor, and the tailor made coats for each of us. Labor was cheap at this time in Austria, and the tailor was glad to have work. And we were glad to have coats!

There was enough fabric remaining to also make three skirts for us girls. These were the coats and skirts we would wear on the ship as we immigrated to the United States—and for many years afterward as well. I was so thankful for God's provision, my dad's ingenuity, and my sister's willingness to work so many hours to clothe us and take care of mom and the household.

Over time, more of our relatives found their way to the Salzburg area. These relatives had not been able to leave when our family left Crvenka. Some of the relatives were from the Banat Region, a short distance away from Crvenka. These relatives, like other ethnic Germans from the Balkans, had been used as forced laborers by the Soviet Union.

One aunt related to us how she and the other workers would place notes in the bottom of the coal carts to be read by the workers at the other end. They developed a method of communication by which both ends learned the names of those who were still in regions of the Balkans; those who had been taken to Russia; and those who had been able to flee to Austria, Germany, or other countries.

Most of those who were deported to the Soviet Union were sent to work in the reconstruction of heavy industry and mines. These deported ethnic Germans were housed in concentration camps, under armed guard. Many died. The Russians learned that this system of forced labor was inefficient and unprofitable since many of the women and older men were not physically able to perform the hard labor that heavy construction or mining required. So the deported ethnic Germans from the Balkans were eventually released and repatriated.

We never heard from some of our relatives who had been deported during this time and have since assumed that they died as prisoners in these labor camps. Again, we were thankful for dad's World War I experiences, which had impressed upon him the need for us to flee from Crvenka and avoid forced labor, deportation, and the many other horrors of being a prisoner.

Late one hot summer night, we were awakened by two American soldiers who suddenly appeared in our kitchen, which was also our sleeping quarters. They had pushed the screens in the window and jumped in. The soldiers did not speak German, but they made a flapping motion with their arms and a cackling sound. We realized that they were wanting eggs. But we did not have any, not one single egg.

During this communication, they overheard my twin's asthmatic, raspy breathing and said, "Child sick; take doctor."

Dad signaled back, rubbing his thumb across the tips of his fingers to say that it would take money that we did not have.

In response, one of the soldiers pulled out his wallet and gave my dad a fifty-dollar American bill. That was a great deal of money. And my twin got to go to the doctor. What an unexpected surprise.

Connecting the Dots . . .

How resourceful are you when presented with an enormous need and no pattern to follow?

One young man, a Romanian psychologist, faced such a need. After World War II, the streets of Europe were filled with orphaned Jewish children. Israel had become a nation, and Dr. Reuven Feuerstein, having trained at the Sorbonne with Piaget, was assigned the task of determining how to train these young minds. He had to prepare these young Jews to participate in a new technological society in Israel. Many of these orphans had never had parental nurturing and had been labeled as uneducable—not able to learn.

When Dr. Feuerstein began to test the youths to form a baseline of their level of cognitive development, he immediately recognized that the standard Intelligence Quotient (I.Q.) testing of that time was worthless. The test was invalid when applied to these children who'd had no consistent structure, attachment, or family culture. Now what?

Dr. Feuerstein believed that man is created in the image of God. Therefore, man has tremendous potential for growth. He coined the concept of neuroplasticity. Dr. Feuerstein believed the brain is capable of structural change. We now recognize this concept as accurate; it's happening all the time. But in 1948, there were no imaging devices to prove this theory.

Dr. Feuerstein went on to define the processes of thinking, or learning to learn. He specifically isolated twenty-six cognitive functions and designed teaching tools used to mediate the development of these functions. His successes were nothing short of miraculous. Many of the youths who were trained with his teaching tools went on to become leaders in the nation of Israel.

Dr. Feuerstein's Instrumental Enrichment tools and his mediated-learning experience concepts are applied today all over the world. On every continent, these tools are changing lives. Dr. Feuerstein was a Jew, and when he was ninety years old, he was still living in Israel and still teaching people how to think. One of the Instrumental Enrichment tools is titled *The Organization of Dots.*

Think about it.

CHAPTER 24

Bittersweet

After what seemed like an eternity, the United States visa approval documents arrived. We had been waiting for six long years and now were filled with great joy and much fear. For some reason, we had never studied the English language and had very limited knowledge of what life in America would be like. We had seen a few films of the rich and famous Americans, which turned out to be rather misleading. When we finally did arrive in America, we realized that the Americans made their soup with water too.

The day after receiving our visas, I went to work and shared the news with Dr. Dittenberger. This was a bittersweet experience. I had come to love and cherish my mentor and his family. Dr. Dittenberger offered to adopt me as his own child and then leave the practice to me. Actually, that sounded pretty good to me at first. I was by then eighteen years of age, and in a few months, I could be recognized as a dentist in Austria.

I rode the bicycle home, excited to share this latest development with my father, all the way rejoicing in the possibility of soon being able to help provide for my parents and family.

I walked into the house, met my dad in the hallway, and shared the news with him. He was not so thrilled. In fact, he looked at me with his clear blue eyes and said, "Would you leave me now?"

I ran from the hall to the outhouse and cried and prayed. I have no idea how long I stayed out there weeping and praying. But that same evening, I asked my father to return with me to Dr. Dittenberger's. I needed Dad's support as I thanked Dr. Dittenberger for his gracious offer. But I also needed to explain to him that I felt my parents needed me with them at this time.

I was so impressed that even after I declined Dr. Dittenberger's offer to stay, he handed me a Hungarian gold piece. We used those to make gold crowns for our patients. So I knew it was very costly.

He handed the costly gold coin to me and said, "Schatzie, this is a symbol of our everlasting friendship that will never rust." He looked at my dad and said, "Forgive me, Ludwig. Please don't blame me for trying to keep your daughter here with us." We hugged and shed more tears. As we turned to depart, he said, "Remember that if things do not work out, you always have a home here with us."

During my first year in the United States, I was tempted to take Dr. Dittenberger up on his offer and return to Austria.

My father was sixty years old, my mom was fifty-three years old, and we would be starting all over again in a new country, with no financial resources. We did not receive any financial reimbursement for our property in Yugoslavia. So what we would start with in America was what we had in our hearts and our minds, plus we had a little debt because we would have to repay our sponsors for the money they had loaned us for travel.

Relationally, it was very difficult to part with our family that still would be in Europe. My sister, her husband, and their two children still remained in Austria and my brother Eduard was staying in Linz, Austria. Then, of course, we had to leave Dr. Ferdinand Dittenberger, his family, and all the many friendships we had cultivated over those six long years in Austria.

Connecting the Dots . . .

Have you ever taken a trip with little knowledge of what you might encounter? Perhaps it was a senior-citizen mystery trip or a mission trip to a third-world country. You know where you're going, but you really have no clue where you will sleep, what you will do, and what you will eat. It is a good idea to always pack a jar of peanut butter and your own toilet paper.

Step into the shoes of a refugee, and try, just try, to imagine what it must feel like to immigrate to an entirely new country, on an entirely new continent, where people speak an entirely different language. And when you speak, your accent is a dead giveaway that you are a foreigner—not just any foreigner, but a foreigner whose native tongue is identified with the cause of a world war. And you don't have any money. But what you do have is in your heart and in your mind. You have perseverance and a solid faith in God. And you have your precious family. What more could you ask for?

Think about it.

CHAPTER 25

A Second Chance and What Did You Say?

In 1951, we came to the United States with the clothes on our backs, God's Word in our hearts, a strong work ethic, and thankful hearts because we were being given a second chance.

We had our visas and passports and had completed our requirements for immigration to the United States by taking an oath stating that none of our family would ever become a burden to the United States government. We promised that we would provide for our own needs in this new land of opportunity. We knew that our dependence would be on God, so we took a train to Bremerhaven and waited for our ship to arrive.

A few weeks later, at the end of February, 1951, we boarded a United States Navy ship, the *General Muir*, at Bremerhaven, Germany. The ship took troops over to Europe and brought refugees/immigrants back to the USA. Our party included my parents, my aunt, my siblings, and me. We had two big trunks, which contained linens, a few clothes, and table service. We also carried on a personal suitcase for immediate use.

There were separate sleeping quarters for the men and the women. Each room contained about a dozen bunk beds. We had to work for our passage fare. My dad and my brother painted the ship with the painting crew. My older sister and I were on the kitchen crew. Due to their health, Mom, my twin, and my aunt were excused from working for passage fare.

The meals were served cafeteria style, and my job was dishing out the food to those in the receiving line. The ship's military personnel were our foremen. My boss was an African American soldier. This was the first time in my eighteen years that I had ever been in the same room with an African American person. He was very kind to us. After I had been working under his supervision for a few days, he began saying the same phrase over and over to me in English. I did not understand what he was saying, so I repeated the phrase as best I could to another refugee girl, who was also working on the ship. She told me that the next time he said that phrase to me, I should respond with, "Just a little."

The next day, when he said that phrase to me, I said, "Just a little." It was odd, but he started giving me special food for my family and me. So I told this to the girl who had fashioned my response. She started giggling. I asked her again what the phrase meant. Then she interpreted for me what his English phrase, "Do you love me?" meant in German. Oh my goodness! I was so embarrassed. But now I knew more English. I also learned the lesson not to respond to any phrases when I did not fully understand the meaning. So I just listened, smiled and did my kitchen work. This kind man even brought us a farewell cake the night before our arrival at Ellis Island.

We were on the ship for thirteen days and had only one detour due to stormy weather. Of course, we had some sea sickness and some wobbly walking when we departed the ship. Thank God for His provision again.

Coming into the harbor and being met by our lady the Statue of Liberty, I was overwhelmed with a flood of emotions. I was filled with hope, relief, fear, gratitude, and exhaustion. I was especially exhausted from the last six years of waiting for this moment.

As we departed the *General Muir*, we passed through a line of the ship's military personnel, who were congratulating us and welcoming us to the United States of America. We had finally arrived in this land of freedom.

Connecting the Dots . . .

If you want to get a sense of how valuable freedom is, try this. The next time you are in any foreign country, walk by the United States Embassy. Notice the tremendous number of people lined up, camping outside the embassy, waiting for admission. They are waiting to gain admission to apply for a visa to the United States. The numbers are often in the hundreds.

The national people can't just walk into the embassy. Why? They are not United States citizens. They do not have a passport. But you do. Walk past the hundreds of faces rounding the block, go to the main doors, and show the guard your passport. Zip, you are in. Just like that, because you have the credentials. Your United States passport allows you admission to almost any country in the world. And what have you done to deserve such a privilege? Value and cherish it, please. Do something so that your passport will retain its waning value.

Think about it.

CHAPTER 26

New Beginnings

When we got off of the *General Muir*, a man who lived in New York and who knew our sponsors from Indiana came to greet us. We went through customs and then boarded a train to the state of Indiana. When we arrived at the train station, our sponsors met us and took us to Francesville, Indiana.

Our sponsors had prepared a dinner for us. There was a green-colored something wiggling on the buffet table. I thought it was alive. I commented to one of the housekeepers, "What is that? Is it alive?"

She started laughing and told me it was Jell-O. That was my first time seeing Jell-O. I sampled a small portion and decided it must be an acquired taste that I had not yet developed.

Everyone was talking to us, welcoming us, but not all of these conversations were in German. In fact, much of the conversation was in English, and we could not understand it. So we just nodded our heads and smiled a lot.

An old house had been rented for us in Francesville. It had two bedrooms and some furnishings. We stayed with some of the church friends the first week as we worked on readying the house for occupation. It was far better than what we had lived in as refugees in Austria. It even had indoor plumbing.

The first year in the United States was another year of huge transition. Our lack of command of the English language caused us to have to work in employment that was far beneath our actual training. But that was fine. By this time in our lives, we had all learned to be content with whatever God provided for us. We were just so thankful for any employment and for the opportunity to start anew in this land of freedom.

For the first few months, I cleaned houses and mowed lawns. Then I was very blessed to find employment with Mrs. Grace Hubbard. I worked as a maid in their home. The Hubbards were beautiful people to work for, and she taught me the English language. Up until that time, my primary learning tool had been looking at children's picture books.

While attending church in Francesville, I met a lady whose dentist in Lafayette needed a dental technician. She drove me down to Lafayette to interview with Dr. Lord, Sr. He hired me to start as soon as possible.

I wanted to give appropriate notice to Mrs. Hubbard, but when she found out that my starting salary was twice my current wage, she encouraged me to start with Dr. Lord immediately. She even gave me a special gift. Again, this was God's hand at work in my life.

Coincidentally, a friend from church in Francesville had a sister who already had rented a room with a Mrs. Weihnhart in Lafayette. The room would easily accommodate two occupants, and it was in walking distance of Dr. Lord's dental office in the Lafayette Life Building.

My father was able to move me into Mrs. Weihnhart's home and meet her. They had a wonderful time talking because she also spoke German. She was so nice to me. She even shared her special baked goodies with me because she knew that I gave my earnings to my parents. Our family was saving all of our earnings to purchase a farm so my dad could start over again as a farmer.

God is so good. He once again provided tangible protection and mentoring for me. Mrs. Weihnhart was like a protecting angel to me, and Dr. Lord was like a second father. Many times, Dr. Lord spoke up in my defense. You see, it was not popular to be German in the United States in 1952. With my accent, it was impossible to deny my heritage. People would loudly comment with disgust, "There goes another kraut who took our job away."

When Dr. Lord heard such comments, he would confront the people and tell them the facts: "Before you even think about getting out of bed in the morning, my girl, Hilda, is already here in the lab and getting ready to assist me for the day. When you are drinking your second martini in the evening, she is still in our office, cleaning up from the day's exams and preparing for the next day's work. She deserves this job." They got the message.

Dr. Lord treated me well and paid me well. In fact, I was known as "Dr. Lord's girl." When I was working for Dr. Lord, it was about the happiest, most carefree time of my life.

After our first year in America, my father rented some land and resumed farming. This property had a house on it, so my family moved into this farmhouse. Each year, my father continued to add some additional rental property, and after a few years, our family purchased a farm, which had a house and farm buildings. That property is still in our family.

I continued to work in Lafayette during the week and would come home on the weekends to help my parents and attend church with them. I also worked at the Saint Elizabeth Hospital as a nurse's aide because my mom needed surgery for her varicose veins. My parents did not have health insurance, so I was working extra to pay for the surgeon's fee. My siblings were paying for the hospital fee. I had half of the fee paid for when, one day, the surgeon, who knew that I worked for Dr. Lord, happened to see me working at the hospital. He asked the head nurse, "What's Hilda doing working here?" The nurse told him why. The next time I went to his office to pay on the account for Mom's surgery, his staff told me that the fee was paid in full. I did not owe anything. Again, God provided through gracious people.

Connecting the Dots . . .

Proverbs 3:27 says, "Do not withhold good from those who deserve it, when it is within your power to act."

What a potentially transforming statement. Certainly this is within the possibility of every human being, rich or poor. From: shoveling the widow's sidewalk, rebuilding a home damaged from a tornado, assisting a child in your church's special needs ministry or encouraging a passerby with a smile, we all have the power to encourage those we encounter in our daily lives. Joining with others who take the mandate seriously, we can provide a godly environment to mentor troubled youth or partner with a ministry that provides physical, emotional and spiritual support to forgotten children and adults around the world.

And we can pray. Prayer is an action verb.

At home or internationally, as a group or independently, it is daily within our power to act, to have the privilege to do good and to be Jesus to someone.

Think about it.

CHAPTER 27

A New Name and a New Citizen

One day, Susie, the receptionist, took a call for me and said, "He sounds nice; you should talk to him." So I did. It was single man, Erven, from our church. Erven's family had immigrated from Crvenka to the United States in 1906. They had been one of the families to sponsor my family's immigration. So we had this common heritage. Erven was very intelligent and could piece the patterns of history together with insightful perspective.

Erven had been attending a Bible college in Chicago with another friend from our church and had recently moved back to the area. He was now attending a university in Lafayette and was calling to ask me for a date. We agreed on a mutual time, and the rest is history. This man later became my husband. But, as with many things in life and even in God's will, it was not smooth, easy, or pain free.

We dated for about a year and set a date for our wedding. We were preparing to order our wedding invitations when we received news that would change our lives forever. My fiancé, when attending the Bible college in Chicago, had taken communion with other Christians there. This was not an accepted practice in our denomination. So, at a member meeting just before our invitations were to be printed, we were excommunicated from our church.

I was devastated, but my fiancé was crushed. This would affect the rest of his life, my life, and the lives of our family members. But God spoke to me through Psalm 57, and I felt that although it was going to be a struggle, I was to honor my commitment to marry Erven.

It had been our habit that when the weather did not permit travel to Francesville, we would attend a Reformed church in Lafayette. When the minister there learned of what had happened to us, he immediately gave his blessing and permission to be married there. And so we were married on June 13, 1959, and I became Mrs. Erven Gutwein.

I resumed my work at Dr. Lord's office. Erven tried to find purpose through his singing quartet and his research about his constant headaches. While serving in the Korean War and jumping from a burning truck, he had suffered damage to his cervical vertebrae. As a result, he suffered from constant pain and headaches. This was a continuous reality. He tried to take pain relievers, but the side effects did not permit him to function well enough to be employed. So we visited specialist after specialist, trying to find a remedy to this chronic pain.

After living in the United States the required number of years, I applied for United States citizenship and began the process of naturalization. Throughout this process, I was required to learn about the history of the United States, her Declaration of Independence, her Constitution, her Bill of Rights, and both the privileges and the responsibilities of living in this land of freedom. Only a godly people who are controlled internally are capable of thriving in a democratic constitutional republic such as ours. The founders of the United States, who had the unique ability to study the history of many governments before establishing ours here, knew this vital fact.

We must be a nation of godly people. As our founders knew, men either control themselves by an inner moral conscience or they are controlled externally by force. I was fully aware of what it was like to be controlled by governments using external force.

I became a citizen of this great nation in the summer of 1961, while I was pregnant with our daughter. To me, this was important. Our child's mother would be a citizen of the United States. All three people in our family would be citizens of the United States of America. After so many years of being called a foreigner, I could proudly respond that I was a full citizen. I had to relinquish my former citizenship of Yugoslavia and promise that I would not become a burden to the United States of America. I pledged to do my duty as a citizen and to do my utmost to uphold the Constitution. I chose and I cherish this nation that is full of people of great diversity—all a part of one nation under God. It was an oath I did not take lightly.

Connecting the Dots . . .

Do you vote in every election? Do you view voting as a privilege or as an inconvenience? Do you diligently research the candidates before you vote? Do you take your children with you so that they can get into the habit?

Have you read the Declaration of Independence lately? Let me refresh your memory. The signers declared these seven truths to be understood by everyone:

1. That all men are created equal under God.
2. That all men are born with rights that no one can take away from them.
3. That some of these rights are life, liberty, and the right to pursue happiness.
4. That the purpose of a government is to preserve these rights for all men.
5. That the government is the servant of the people and gets its powers with the permission of the people it governs.
6. That, if a government fails to protect people's rights, the people have the right and the duty to change government.
7. That men have the right to form new governments that will protect their rights and to provide safety and happiness.

Do you see some discrepancies between what our founding fathers declared and what is currently taking place in our nation?

Read the Constitution and the Bill of Rights. Help your children to understand the value of these documents. They are well thought out. With an unprecedented opportunity to birth a nation, our founding fathers were able to create a new form of government that was designed to avoid the tragic paths that curse human history.

The Constitution and the Bill of Rights were formed to provide a cage around the federal government. The founders knew from experience that the tendency was for governments to become increasingly more powerful, eventually centralizing power in a dictator, king, or totalitarian form. The Constitution and Bill of Rights were created to restrain the government from doing this. If the door of the cage was left open, watch out. The ravenous beast of government would be let loose, and history, yet again, would repeat itself for lack of a thinking, diligent people keeping the Constitutional cage intact.

Think about it.

CHAPTER 28

My Little Sunshine

We were awaiting the birth of our first child. The pregnancy went well, but the delivery was another story. After I had been in labor for forty-two hours, I was very weak. At that point, it was getting to be a life or death situation for both the baby and me.

I later found out that our daughter was turned posterior, with her head pressing against my pelvic bone. The doctor had figured this out, but he had five other patients in labor and did not pay enough attention to me. When the nurse who had attended me the previous day came back on shift and saw that I was still there and still in labor, she was livid. She told the doctor that she would not leave her shift until my baby was delivered. She rounded up all the necessary staff to bring the delivery about. She even found a lady doctor who worked at the Arnett Clinic whose hand was small enough to reach in and turn my child around so that she could come out through the birth canal.

So, when I first saw our daughter, she did not seem to have a forehead. I remarked about this deformity to the doctor, and he assured me that my daughter would be fine. I was the one he was concerned about. He said that I should not get pregnant again, and if I did, I should never come to him for obstetrics care.

I was so thankful for God's provision of the courageous nurse who helped to save both my child and me. I asked her what I could do for her. She asked only to dress my baby for her home going. So the nurse got to dress our daughter, Dawn Elaine.

My baby became the sunshine of my life. Now my parents were also grandparents. So from now on, I will refer to them as Otie *(GrossVater)* and Omie *(GrossMutter)*.

I went back to working for Dr. Lord. Dawn went to childcare. Erven continued to suffer. A specialist suggested a change of climate, like a desert. So I quit my wonderful job with Dr. Lord, and we moved to San Diego, California, hoping the change would relieve some of Erven's pain. Dawn was one year old when we moved.

We purchased an insulation business, but after a year, Erven's headaches had not subsided. So with no extended family living there and Dawn now a toddler, we sold the business on contract, which later was defaulted upon, and moved back to Lafayette.

We had no money, so I needed to find work. God knew this. God sent me to a Howard Johnson's restaurant. I had no restaurant experience, but they were short of help and hired me. I started working there the next day. I was a waitress trainee for one day, a waitress on my own for the next few days, and by the end of the week, I was cashier/ hostess. Within a year, I was the restaurant manager.

Dawn and I would drive up to Francesville and visit Otie and Omie about once a month. We would sing along the way and stop for a frozen custard too. Although I could not sing like my husband, I made a joyful noise, and it stuck, because Dawn still recounts the songs with a giggle and a tear. I sang songs such as "Onward Christian Soldiers," "On Christ the Solid Rock I Stand," "A Mighty Fortress is Our God," and German songs like *"Es Giebt ein Wunder Schönes Land woh Reine Freude Wohnt, Wo Hass und Hader sind verbant . . . weil dort die Liebe Thront"* ("There is a beautiful land where pure joy reigns, where hatred and greed are banished, because love reigns there").

Now, of course, Dawn had not yet received formal training in the German language. So she would just repeat the words the way they sounded to her and make her own meaning. As Dawn grew older, she would help Otie go shopping in the small store in town; she was so proud to be his helper. Otie had learned some English but appreciated his spunky, redheaded granddaughter going to help him.

Omie would have a list of items to make cookies, and although Omie did not speak English, Dawn and she communicated beautifully. Dawn learned some German words too. Well, not very much German, as she later found out in college. Dawn thought she could test out of German, but alas, she did not, because what she had been absorbing with Otie and Omie and our family was not only Hoch German, but also it had Hungarian and Schwäbisch mixed in. She wondered, "Which word for potato do I choose? *Krumpberra? Erdäpfel? Kartoffeln?*" So she did end up taking a few years of German in college. This was great for us when we needed to communicate around non-German speakers, and it was helpful in our later businesses.

Connecting the Dots...

God bless grandparents! God please especially bless those grandparents who are faithfully involved in their grandchildren's lives.

To grandparents, I say this: Your families need you, our nation needs you. Your time to teach is now. Teach us now before the history books write you out of history and your truths are forever locked away. Speak up, counsel, and share your wisdom with us. And pray for us. It may be that we shall soon envy you.

Think about it.

CHAPTER 29

Hope and Another Profession

About this time, Erven's brother, who was an orthopedic surgeon, learned of a surgeon in Canada who was developing a technique to replace the crushed cervical vertebrae in an individual's neck. This was a new procedure, not yet available in the United States. And while offering hope, it entailed a great amount of risk. There was a fifty percent chance of success. If unsuccessful, Erven could be left a quadriplegic or paraplegic.

By this time, improvements in medical imaging were able that confirmed that his headaches were coming from crushed vertebrae. Those images confirmed that there was indeed an organic cause of his headaches. These crushed 3, 4, and 5 cervical vertebrae were pressing on the nerves, causing tremendous pain. The pain was constant and increasing in severity. In fact, the surgeon later remarked that it was a miracle that Erven remained sane through all the intense pain.

The procedure for fixing the vertebrae was extremely high-risk, with multiple surgeries. It was possible that I would not only need to support our family but also need to take care of Erven. So we decided that I should study for a license in cosmetology so that I could work from our home should it be necessary.

On Dawn's first day of kindergarten, I began my first day of cosmetology school. We renovated a room in our home to be a beauty shop, complete with equipment. It took about five years for all of the preparations to be completed. During the two years it took me to become licensed in cosmetology, I continued to work at Howard Johnson's as a hostess or waitress. God continued to provide work for me, and the owners of Howard Johnson's graciously continued to provide our family with health insurance.

Erven underwent testing and preparations in anticipation of the surgery. His brother even flew in to observe/assist during the first surgery, which took place in Toronto, Canada. Of course, I was there too. We were there for only a week before the doctors advised us to take Erven home early. There was a nurses' strike going on in Canada at that time, and the doctors were fearful that he would not receive adequate care in the hospital. So we flew back to Indiana, and I nursed Erven from our home.

Praise God! The first surgery was a complete success. There was a decrease in pain, and there were no other side effects other than some loss in Erven's ability to turn his neck. These new vertebrae, fashioned from his femur bone, were somehow fused and did not pivot as the natural ones do. Since the surgery was a success, I did not need to work as a cosmetologist from our home. So I continued working in the restaurant industry, Erven continued to recuperate, and Dawn continued her studies.

I am so thankful that God always provided me with good employment, but I do regret that I was not able to be a stay-at-home mother for Dawn. I just felt that I had to provide for our family. I had taken that oath that neither I nor my family would ever be dependent on the government.

While I was working and unable to fill my motherly role in the typical fashion, Erven assumed the role of educational mediator for Dawn. He challenged her to think and look for truth. He taught her to read and gave her regular research assignments to supplement her education. Erven enjoyed making people think and was well suited for this role of helping with Dawn's cognitive development.

The restaurant industry demands long hours, and there were several tasks that Erven was very gifted at helping with. He was good at problem solving and developing methods for efficiency, organization, and bookkeeping. Erven was also very proficient at the ongoing demands of equipment and facility maintenance that accompany any restaurant venue. So when a restaurant and motel in northern Indiana became available for purchase, we bought it. Our family had frequented it for years, and it was closer to the community in which our extended family lived, so in the fall of 1975, we relocated to Winamac, Indiana.

The first few months, we were in training with the previous owners. And within the first month, Erven had an appendix attack. The doctor, knowing I needed to manage the restaurant, took him to the hospital himself. He told me to get the lunch served and assured me that he would take care of Erven. The doctor was such a kind man.

In 1976, we had another major event. That year, my parents passed away within three weeks of each other. At their funeral, Dawn sang, *"Es Gibt Ein Wunder Schönes Lande . . ."* one of the songs we had sung together on our drives up to visit them. Even weeks after their passing, out of habit, I would go to the phone to call Omie or Otie to ask a question or to check up on them.

Life was hard, but God continued to give us what we needed to stay afloat; although, many days it seemed we were just barely afloat. Owning and operating a restaurant with two floors, seating for 200, two kitchens, and two bars, plus a motel with twenty rooms and forty beds, is a 24/7 job. Most days started before 6 A.M., and last call in the downstairs bar was at 1 A.M. Whenever I got a day off, I would sleep. Or once in a while, Erven would encourage Dawn and me to take a shopping adventure to Logansport or even to Lafayette. He was very generous to us, knowing that we both needed to "get out" and that we both enjoyed pretty clothes.

In January of 1978, when I was in California for my twin sister's wedding, I got a call from Dawn, who was back home in Winamac. Dawn had planned to accompany me to the wedding but had come down with a virus, so she stayed home. She was then sixteen years old.

Dawn said weakly, "Mom, hurry home; I'm dying . . ." She said she had been drinking fluids all weekend, but she was still very thirsty and had gotten dehydrated and lost over twenty pounds. Erven, while also managing the restaurant and motel, had done his best to care for Dawn, but she continued to get worse.

My brother and I caught the first available flight home. When we arrived, the weather in Indiana was bitterly cold.

I walked into the house and found that Dawn was nearly unconscious.

She was sitting on a chair and trying to get to the restroom. I knelt down in front of her and prayed for God to spare her life, saying, "Please save her; she's just a blossom. Take me instead."

I quickly grabbed the phone and dialed a phone number I did not even know. God did the dialing; it was a miracle. It was for the EMS, and I told them to come to The Indian Head, the name of our business. The house we were renting at this time was adjacent to the back parking lot of the restaurant property.

At the hospital, they started an I.V. I asked if they had begun blood testing, and the physician responded that they had not but that they had checked the urine and it was just a bad cold.

I demanded that they check Dawn's blood for glucose. When the results came back, the physician came rushing back into the room and yanked out the I.V. He was white as a sheet, even though he was of Indian descent. He said, "Oh my, glucose is 900 mg/dl!" Then he left.

Dawn had been unconscious ever since leaving the house and continued to be so. I took her hand and just began to pray. From working in the hospital in Lafayette, I knew that blood sugar that high was not good. That was on a Sunday.

My brother-in-law, the surgeon, came the next day from Lafayette, driving through the beginnings of what has come to be recorded as "the blizzard of 1978." He told me to be realistic, that Dawn likely would be a "vegetable," not regaining full mental faculties. That type of blood sugar level was thought to cause a certain amount of brain damage.

The initial physician stayed in the hospital around the clock and came into Dawn's room every hour on the hour and asked her two questions: "What is your name? How old are you?" Since Dawn was still unconscious, she did not respond.

I stayed and slept in a chair in her room and carried on a one-way conversation with her and a two-way conversation with God.

By now, the blizzard was in full force. The restaurant and motel were packed with stranded travelers. Even people who did not know one another were sharing the same rooms. Erven was able to get a ride on a snowmobile to say "hi" and stay for a short visit before returning to the business. The physician still continued to make his hourly visits with his same two questions.

Finally, on Wednesday afternoon when the doctor came in and asked his two questions, Dawn responded with frustration, "Dawn Elaine Gutwein, age sixteen." To her, it seemed he had been annoying her with those interrogations since forever, but up to that point, she just could not respond to them.

The storm subsided, and some of Dawn's classmates came and brought her a big teddy bear. I was so relieved but continued to stay with her as she learned how to be a teenager with a recent diagnosis of juvenile diabetes: daily injections, meal planning, and having to think before doing lots of things. It was a new challenge, but we were just so thankful that Dawn had not suffered any brain damage.

God is so merciful, hearing and answering the tender pleas of a mother and many other praying friends.

Connecting the Dots . . .

Sometimes God allows illness to make us dependent on Him. That's a good thing. We can quickly realize how very fragile we truly are as human beings. Without Him, we are nothing.

Sometimes God also gives warnings to nations to humble them, to bring them to repentance, to wake up the people of a nation, and to draw the hearts of men to His. Surely God has been doing that with the people of the United States. We seem to have been roused with the events of 9/11, but we quickly resumed our slumber.

How many times will God try to awaken our nation before it is too late? We are not so patient ourselves. If you were God, how long would you put up with our blatant sins?

It's our turn to choose. The Bible teaches, "If my people, who are called by my name, will humble themselves and pray and seek my face and turn from their wicked ways, then will I hear from heaven and will forgive their sin and will heal their land" (2 Chronicles 7:14).

Think about it.

CHAPTER 30

Drought, Darkness, Deliverance, and Healing

Economic times continued to plague our small business, and since we were working eighteen-hour days, seven days a week, for many years with no relief, the strain was hard to escape. This led to great stress in our marriage as well. Eventually, it became necessary for Erven and me to separate.

Marriage is like a flower. It requires tender, thoughtful attention and constant care—healthy soil; a safe, nurturing environment; and refreshing air. It requires daily watering and the vital warmth of faithful friends and family. We need sunshine and rest, and lots of *Son* shine. The entire marriage plant must be growing in Christ, reaching ever deeper for His living water. Marriage must be branching ever upward, putting forth more leaves to absorb His power to grow healthy and more able to withstand the drought, heat, and storms of life.

Although I knew at the beginning of my marriage that my husband was spiritually wounded, I had hoped that in time this wound would heal. It did not. The excommunication from our church denomination just prior to our marriage and the shunning that we, and our families, had experienced had caused deep wounds. Erven had felt forsaken by many of his life-long friends and perhaps even by God. For Erven, these wounds did not heal. It was hard for me, but I had experienced so many Christian denominations and so many transitions during my youth in Europe that I was better able to move forward in my faith. I knew to focus on Christ and not on His children. Men are men, and they make mistakes. I was able to forgive and go on. This was not so easy for Erven.

As time, storms, and responsibilities increased, my stem and growing roots alone were not enough to support our marriage. A faithful body of Christians came to help support us, pray, and protect us. But alas, by that time, some of the roots had become too dry to be receptive to help. Our marriage plant toppled. So, at the counsel of clergy, friends, and professionals, a separation was made. Papers were filed, and our property was placed on sale.

I still question what I could have done differently to save our marriage. I question whether or not our marriage would have thrived if Erven had had a faithful male mentor, a close accountability partner to help him overcome the hurts he harbored, and friends to see into the real challenges of our lives. But being in the public eye, we often had to present a happy face when all was not happy. At the end, people did try, but it was too late.

Perhaps this will help some of you who may be struggling. Cultivate the godly relationships that help to mentor your marriage and provide the accountability that we all need. Do not attempt to live in isolation, sheltering the truth from those who could help bring healing. Pray, and seek professional insight as a healthy maintenance plan, not merely when the marriage is showing signs of distress or worse.

Despite this tragedy with our marriage, God's hand was undeniably obvious as we attempted to sell all our properties. Despite horrible economic times for properties such as ours, our business sold—all of it. The restaurant, the motel, and our home all sold. And it all sold within the necessary timeframe—necessary, because if it had not sold, it would have been placed in a forced sale auction, providing little or no return for all our years of hard labor that ultimately cost us our marriage. After the closing, even my attorney said, "This truly was a miracle of God."

By this time Dawn, who had continued to come home to work weekends as much as possible, had completed both her undergraduate studies at Purdue and her graduate school studies at Indiana University. So, by the first week of May in 1988, we were full of closure. Dawn graduated from optometry school; we had sold our restaurant, motel, and house; and the divorce was decreed. I say "decreed" because in my heart, I never divorced my husband. We moved what few tangible belongings we had left to my brother's farm in Francesville, back where I first began life in the United States. Erven then went to live with his parents.

Dawn and I took a mission trip to Haiti with our pastor and his wife. Then I boxed up a few items and sent them to my twin's home in California. I would reside with her and her husband until Dawn completed her residency at West Point. My twin and her husband were so gracious, opening their home to me and helping to heal the wounds of my heart.

I accompanied Dawn to West Point, and I was able to meet the couples who would continue to mentor her spiritually and educationally. I met the officers in charge of her residency program.

The captain in charge of her training, sensing Dawn's preciousness to me, put his arm around me and assured me by saying, "Mom, just go on. We will take care of her. Don't you worry."

And they did. Those families adopted and prayed for our family and continue to do so. Dawn was able to live with one of the families and observe firsthand what a Christ-centered marriage looks like. These couples continue to mentor us from afar.

While I was at West Point, we were able to attend the officers' prayer breakfasts. What other nation can say "One nation under God" and know that God has been our foundation from the start? It was inspiring to witness these godly men and women in the leadership of our nation's military seeking God's direction in their lives and in the lives of the cadets they teach, as well as in our nation.

I hold in the utmost esteem all those in the military who make such huge personal sacrifices to preserve liberty and freedom in our United States. Having come from a war zone, knowing the cost of freedom and choosing to be identified as an American, I can comprehend the value of freedom. More than most Americans, I cherish this privilege.

While Dawn was in optometry school at Indiana University, she was a member of a group of Christian optometry students there. These precious friends upheld her there and had prayed for us during our trials of the previous years. The founder of this group of Christian optometrists was a professor there, a godly man for whom we all have the utmost respect.

When Dawn realized that God still wanted her to consider returning to Indiana, she contacted this godly man for his guidance in finding a Christian optometry practice in Indiana. He told Dawn that he knew of just the doctor. In fact, the doctor he was recommending, Dawn's contact, was expecting twins and seeking an associate soon. So we moved to Bluffton. Dawn joined the practice there, and soon we both were adopted by the doctor's family as well.

God is so good to place the lonely in families. This doctor has been a godsend to us both. That doctor was just the mentor and sister that Dawn needed. God has blessed us beyond measure by giving us this family and the community. We thank Him again for His healing provision.

Connecting the Dots . . .

Keep your marriage healthy. Find ways to strengthen the foundations and fortify the walls. The family, instituted by God, is the solid rock of a nation. When the family falls, the nation can fall too.

Be intentional about how you daily demonstrate that you love and respect your mate. Think about what is best for your marriage before you act. Don't just seek your own wants or desires.

Also realize that your godly example will set the model for your children. Your marriage is the only one your children see up close.

Think about it.

CHAPTER 31

Insight and Reconciliation

Shortly after we relocated to Bluffton, I was working in a bakery and slipped and fell on the floor. I hit my head against the display counter and got a concussion. Then I started having terrible headaches that kept increasing in intensity—so much so that I finally returned to the medical office to get help. Pain has to be pretty severe for me to seek medical help.

A nurse encouraged the doctor to request an imagining scan. Thank goodness for those nurses again. They discovered that I had a brain tumor. It was a parietal lobe meningioma, which was about the size of a tennis ball. What to do? We prayed.

The tumor was soon removed by a well-known neurosurgeon of German heritage and was found to be benign. Thank God for His faithful care and for providing just the right professionals and support to bring about His plan.

Shortly after my recovery from my brain-tumor surgery, Dawn received a telephone call from a college friend of hers who was living in Texas. Her friend, also a committed Christian, was in many ways a "big sister" to Dawn during their graduate-school years. Dawn's friend was excited to say that she was now attending a wonderful church in Plano, Texas. The pastor was from Indiana, and he said he knew Dawn's family. His name was Gene Getz. Dawn and her friend, both at the same time, verbalized this godly man's name. Gene had been Erven's best friend from Francesville. In fact, Erven had chosen Dawn's middle name after the name of Gene's wife, Elaine. He and Erven had attended the same Bible college in Chicago together, and even though Erven had to quit the college, Gene went on to graduate. As a pastor, he had started evangelical churches. He also had become a prolific writer and a professor at a prominent Dallas seminary.

Dawn and her friend, also an optometrist, arranged to meet in Texas and to get together with Gene and his wife. They knew of our family situation and said they had some insights they thought were very important for us to know.

During this visit, Erven's friend was able to unlock the mystery surrounding my husband's decision to quit the Bible college and why he was still so wounded. My husband, after more than thirty years, had never told Dawn or me the reason behind this severance from what he had felt was his God-given calling. These insights were a priceless gift, helping us to comprehend the deep sorrow that continued to shadow Erven's life. It was as if he had been a butterfly trying to get out of a cocoon. Yet his wings had been crushed; he was not able to fully take flight. Gene also provided many resources, some of which he had authored, which helped us to more fully understand why the events had left such a deep wound in Erven's life and what emotions had been driving some of his behaviors for so many years.

The lessons we learned from this time were huge. We saw that a person who is in a position of leadership in his family or church must be certain that what he is teaching or condoning is based on the truth of God's Scripture and not merely on the traditions of men. Traditions, like the culture, change over time. But God's truth does not change. James 3:1 says, "Not many of you should presume to be teachers, my brothers, because you know that we who teach will be judged more strictly." We have to be certain that our salvation depends on our relationship with Christ alone, not on the approval of others or a list of religious works.

A few months later, our second mission trip to Haiti was cancelled due to a government coup going on in the country. Since Dawn had the week scheduled off, she approached me, feeling impressed that we needed to go visit her dad and ask for forgiveness if we had hurt him in any way. We needed to do our part in reconciliation. The insights we had learned from Erven's childhood and Bible-college friend had helped us to better understand why Erven had always challenged Dawn to look for the truth. He challenged her to research and find the truth for herself, not just accept at face value what others said.

We had not contacted Erven since the divorce. He was living with his mother in Francesville. I immediately agreed, also feeling this need myself. I just said, "Let's not call ahead," because I was concerned that he would purposely leave if he knew ahead of time that we were coming.

That same day, we drove to Francesville and showed up unannounced. Grandma opened the door with open arms and a surprised countenance. Erven excused himself to go outside, and Grandma took us aside and exclaimed, "He was just saying this morning that if you girls had ever loved him like you said you did, then why weren't you here. And here you are." She hugged us with tears of joy.

Grandma made us a beautiful lunch, over which we asked Erven's forgiveness and we all shared our hearts and motivations for our behaviors. He was touched. And we all parted with lighter hearts now that there was reconciliation. We knew, without a doubt, that this was from God.

Our God is a God of reconciliation. Just as He sent His Son to reconcile mankind to Himself, so also He wants His children to reconcile and forgive each other. In fact, the Scriptures state that we must forgive to be forgiven: "For if you have forgiven men when they sin against you, your heavenly Father will also forgive you. But if you do not forgive men their sins, your Father will not forgive your sins" (Matthew 6:14–15).

Connecting the Dots . . .

Is there anyone you need to forgive? Is there anyone you have offended whose forgiveness you need to ask for? Pray about it. Act on it. You will feel so much better for it. And so will that person. Our God is all about reconciliation, and He will bless our efforts.

Think about it.

CHAPTER 32

The Blessing and More Blessings

After recuperating from my brain-tumor surgery, it was recommended that I have a complete physical. As a result of this exam, I was diagnosed with breast cancer. So there was more to pray about.

Six weeks after our visit to Erven, my sisters and niece came to help us determine how to approach my recent diagnosis of breast cancer. Dawn and her optometry partner had picked up my twin from the airport the day before.

On the morning of March 6, 1991, the phone rang at our home. My twin picked it up. It was for Dawn. It was my sister-in- law, Erven's sister and Dawn's aunt. She told Dawn that her father had just died of a heart attack. The last words Erven had said were, "Tell Dawn that I love her." Little did we know that that reconciliation lunch just six weeks before would be the last time we would see Erven alive on earth.

I underwent a successful lumpectomy and radiation treatment to the affected area. Again, God provided faithful friends to transport me to treatments, encourage, and pray with us throughout this time.

As I aged, knowing all that Dawn and I had experienced, I prayed for a godly man to be her husband. He needed to be a godly man who would understand our hardships and be a protector, respected leader, and sensitive companion so that she would not be alone when I leave this earth. I prayed for one whom I could call "son." After all that we had been through, Dawn and I were, and still are, "a packaged deal."

Again, God answered my prayers perfectly and brought Jim. Dawn, by this time, had decided it was much better to be single and content than married and discontent. She was willing to wait until God had her and her future husband ready, if it was His will for her to marry at all.

One day Dawn came home from work and exclaimed, "I've just had my faith confirmed that there are still some single, Christian men out there who seem normal, who like music, and, and, and . . ."

And so, Dawn and Jim married. Now I have both a daughter and a son. And then I was also blessed to be a grandma. Now my name is "Nana." I have a beautiful little granddaughter named Ellie!

Ellie always says to me, "You love me, don't you, Nana?"

And I say, "I love you, my little sugar."

I pray for Ellie, my precious granddaughter, that God may always be her Solid Fortress and Tender Friend and that she may always hear the voice of Jesus calming her with His love.

Connecting the Dots...

Intercessory prayer helps to explain why God has allowed my life to hold all the varied experiences that it has. All these many trials and experiences, some hard, bitter, and traumatic, also were redeemed by Him. He was and is my Solid Fortress and Tender Friend. Life is all about relationship. God provides and permits experiences in our lives for us to be able to relate to those around us and to reveal His Faithfulness.

I have found this to be true in my life. I can weep with those who weep and rejoice with those who rejoice. I find that I am able to discern a need when others may not seem to notice. I intercede in prayer for others while recalling the physical, spiritual and emotional struggles I have experienced and how God responded to my pleas. I am also able to listen, share and relate my experiences with the validity of having been there too. I believe my testimony holds greater validity since I have experienced so much challenge and so much of God's obvious faithfulness.

These experiences have given me a certain credibility with others and firsthand insights about God's comfort that He speaks about in His Word. Scripture says, "Praise be to the God and Father of our Lord Jesus Christ, the Father of compassion and the God of all comfort, who comforts us in all our troubles, so that we can comfort those in any trouble with the comfort we ourselves have received from God" (2 Corinthians 1:3–4).

I have found it true that God does, without a doubt, work all things together for good in His time. I also have learned that we will be privileged to see His purposes unfold in our lives and in the lives of those around us if we are expectantly watching for His hand in all things. We will often see, as we connect the dots, why He has allowed us to go through certain experiences and how He has redeemed them for good.

I challenge you to look for God's faithfulness in your life. Remember His faithfulness in the past, and watch for His faithfulness each day for the rest of your life. You will not be disappointed.

Think about it.

CHAPTER 33

God's Not Done with Me Yet!

God has a way of calling my attention to something He wants me to do. For some time, I have felt that I needed to write my personal history on paper. Over the years, when folks would catch a glimpse of my past, they would comment, "Hilda, you should write a book."

But not all of my memories are pleasant, and I did not want to dig them up again. After all, I had tucked them away and would only venture to review those memories when something would remind me of an incident or someone would ask me to recount such and such. Yet, more and more, as current events remind me of my youth, I have felt compelled to open the door of my past and bring it to light, in hopes that it will honor God and serve our future generations.

God got my attention and provided the time for me to get my memories on paper in an unusual manner. One morning, while getting out of bed at 6 A.M. to take my doggie outside, I felt a sharp pain course through my entire body. I collapsed on the floor at the side of my nightstand. I lay there praying and praying and calling out for help for the next eleven hours. My poor doggie, Peaches, kept running back and forth, trying to get help somehow. I was in excruciating pain and could not move. I checked my cognition and my limbs. I could tell I had not had a stroke or a heart attack. But I could not move my right leg. I was certain it was broken.

I kept praying and listening and praying and hoping. I was thinking of how soldiers must feel, wounded and waiting, praying for someone to find them. At 4:20 P.M., I earnestly prayed that God would grant my petition to send someone to find me soon. I was going in and out of consciousness. I knew that unless someone found me soon, I would not hear him or her and be able to call for the person to come look for me in the bedroom.

I knew that Dawn would call me at 8 P.M. She had begun calling me every evening while she was in college and has continued to do so all these years. If I did not answer the phone, she would then call the neighbors to come look for me. Or she would drive down to Bluffton to look for me herself. But I knew that by the time Dawn found me, it would be very, very late, and it would be even later by the time I could get to the hospital. Yet I prayed that God's will would be done.

Shortly before 5 P.M., I heard a voice. It was our faithful neighbor who usually took Peaches for a walk in the evening. She had a key and would just get Peaches from the kitchen. Now Peaches, after having relieved herself, was trying to get our neighbor to come to the bedroom and see what had happened to me. Thank God she did. My precious neighbor quickly called her husband, a police officer, and they called the ambulance. Then they called Dawn for me. They helped me get registered into the hospital and stayed with me and Dawn until my surgeon confirmed that I did have a fractured femur. I now call my neighbors "My Rescue Angels."

My femur was totally broken off and displaced two inches overlapping the other segment. I had also lost a great deal of blood. Our pastor came and prayed with us. We all thanked God that I had been found.

I underwent surgery the following morning. The doctor placed rods and pins in my leg. Thank God the surgeon is also a trusted friend, so I could rest assured in his professional intervention and guidance for continued care. For the next three months, I recuperated, relearning to walk. And I prayed a lot.

During this attention-getting time, with my wings clipped, I could not run and do my volunteer work or be around people, which is my life blood. So God brought precious friends to visit me. One friend, interested in my past, volunteered to begin putting my story on paper for us. She knew Dawn and I had wanted to do this. But with Dawn's full plate, we just had not gotten it done. We are so thankful for this special friend's willingness to help us get started.

As current events continued to worsen, flashbacks from my youth continued to mount, so Dawn and I both sensed an urgency to get this book out. Out of necessity, we cleared our schedules and began in earnest. One memory led to another, and the result is my story. I hope that it will somehow draw people to Jesus and open their eyes to His perfect love and faithful provision.

I hope that it will also make people think. I hope it will encourage people to teach their children to think, to view everything in the light of God's purposes and plans. May readers see every event as an opportunity to trust Him more. He is faithful. His faithfulness is written on the pages of humankind, in the pages of Scripture, and on the tablet of my heart. I pray that it will be written on your heart also.

Connecting the Dots...

Think through these insights from the past and choose wisely how to respond while you still have the opportunity to choose—before it is too late and we find ourselves repeating the errors of history.

And remember, no matter what, look to Jesus. I always say, "He's always faithful. He's never early, but He's never late."

Think about it.

CHAPTER 34

Thoughts for Thinkers

To my readers: I hope that you have been able to perhaps identify with someone in our story. The roles and challenges that they faced may be some of yours too.

Perhaps you are a:

- *Father.* You must intentionally prepare your children to defend themselves and to thrive in a hostile culture. As head of the family, you must take the leadership and train your children in the truth of God.
- *Mother* who needs to nurture your children and provide a balance to the outside threats of the world, recognizing the specific needs of each of your children. You need to model the character of a godly woman and be your husband's confidante, helpmate, and right arm.
- *College student* and are being bombarded with new philosophies and old ideologies wrapped in new theories. You are eager to make a difference in the world. You are looking for a place to fit and a cause to uphold. You want a mentor worth following. Study the Standard by which you will measure truth. God's Word. Seek out friendships and mentors that will model, challenge and encourage you to deepen your relationship with Christ. Stand firm knowing that God's wisdom is unchanging and you have found your Solid Rock amidst the shifting sands of the times.

- *Grandparent.* Realize that there is no such thing as retirement. A grandparent's job is never done. You hold the wisdom of the ages. You should recognize the patterns of behavior and the emotions that drive those behaviors. You should spot the trends and point your heirs to the solid foundation by which they can discern truth from deception. And you should model a life of faith, pointing them to God's instruction manual so that they can find His answers for themselves.

- *Child* who has been forced to grow up all too quickly. You are observing and sensing things. You are seeking safety and protection, nurture, attachment, and stability. You need a solid fortress in which to find shelter from the assault of activities and pressures swirling like a storm around you. You need a place to think, a place to begin your foundation, and someone to trust and to take your hand; you need a source of hope for your future.

- *Pastor, teacher, or leader,* and you have a flock looking to you for direction. You need to answer these questions: Are you leading from the front, thinking before you lead? Are you teaching your flock the solid truth? Are you teaching them how to find truth themselves and not be merely dependent on you? Whom are you following yourself?

- *Servant.* You may be in the service of a bad boss or under ungodly leadership that you don't respect, but you need to work. You must live somewhere. Or perhaps you are a servant willing to foster a refugee, adopt a child, or come alongside a single parent or a person needing a friend. Or perhaps you are willing to mentor a young person who is looking for mediation and searching for truth. Don't miss the opportunity to make a difference in someone's life.

No matter what your role or title is, to all of you we say, "Look to Jesus. Truth is in the Book."

CHAPTER 35

Understand the Times

The Bible teaches us in Proverbs 27:12, "The prudent see danger and take refuge, but the simple keep going and suffer for it."

We need to recognize when a culture is on a path heading toward the default of a dictator, monarch, or centralized power. Centralized power is the default pattern of history throughout the ages. We also need to recognize when a people are susceptible and vulnerable and when they are looking for deliverance, protection, and security. People may be seeking a guarantee of provision and be ripe for a charismatic, energetic leader to save or redeem them. And if such a leader comes along, we need to ask if that leader is someone who provides vision and just the rhetoric in which to place hope or someone we can really believe in.

It is also important to recognize when a people are no longer governed by a moral conscience and when they are prone to manipulation and control. We must pay attention when a significant majority only boast of the liberty to perform an act and do not consider the consequences of their actions.

We must recognize a crisis or threat created or perpetuated by propaganda to instill fear and a need for governmental "protection." Watching for a perceived need for dependence on a central power and its military is also important.

When we think about the government, we need to recognize that it has no resources and no money of its own, except that which it takes from its people, conscripts, or borrows from another. It may then redistribute those resources as it sees fit to gain the allegiance of the recipients, who then will relinquish their own freedom in exchange for dependence on the government central power. It is important to watch out for deception and propaganda, the subliminal techniques of mass marketing. We need to be alert to the subtle and the sensational, the emotional and the visual. We need to verify things and search many sources so that we will not be in such a hurry to blindly accept everything we hear, see, or read. Also, we should not feast on every piece of media that is available. Before we indulge and intentionally or unintentionally let any deception take up residence in our minds and hearts, we must see how it measures up to God's truth. If it does not measure up to God's truth and standards, we should not allow it influence in our lives.

In the media, we need to recognize censorship, deceptive concepts, and false ideologies that are woven into the education of young people and presented as scientific truth. Know what the children are being taught and exposed to by the media and educators at all levels.

We also need to recognize the infringement upon the nation's Constitution. There currently are pseudo-science claims of ideologies based on science that are being presented as truth. Any time there is a vision that is proclaiming a new man or a new order, be alert, especially if a utopian-type change that justifies brutality to accomplish its establishment is being promoted. Also recognize when a message, philosophy, or media report does not align with inner moral conscience. Recognize that a democratic constitutional republic in which the citizenry has a vote is a rare form of government in the annals of history, and it should be preserved and protected.

As we watch what's going on around us, we must remember that most republics are destroyed from within, not from an enemy nation. It is the headiness of prosperity that eventually leads to moral decay. Then while mired in moral decay, people lose sight of the virtues upon which their republic was founded. Sinking ever deeper, some allow themselves to be manipulated, fed, and entertained by a dictator, Caesar, or Czar who usurps their freedoms and their former independence and makes them dependent on his bureaucracy. It's all about control, not about the well-being of the populace. Review the history of nations, and recognize the patterns.

In addition to all this, it is critical that we recognize why freedom is so rare. Why is it so highly prized by most of the world's citizenry but rarely obtained? Find out what is required to maintain freedom in a nation. Then decide if you think freedom is worth the effort. If you value your freedom and the hope of freedom for your heirs, then do your part to preserve this freedom. Do your duty to build upon the foundation; then repair and maintain the walls. Think, pray, and act. And teach your children to do so too.

Think about it. Now it's your turn to choose.

> It is for freedom that Christ has set us free. Stand
> firm, then, and do not allow yourselves to be burdened
> again by a yoke of slavery. (Galatians 5:1)

PHOTOGRAPHS

Father, Ludwig Welker serving in WW I in the Austrian- Hungarian Balloon Corps, the "Luftfahrtruppen" called "the Imperial and Royal Aviation Troops", note the balloon insignia on his collar.

Mother, Luisa Koch (Welker), marriage engagement photo

Father, Ludwig Welker III, seated on the wagon and one of Hilda's brothers, harvesting at the farm, photo taken in the mid 1930's.

Mother, Luisa Koch Welker, mother of eight children, photo taken circa 1938

Ludwig Welker IV, Hilda's oldest brother, in his Hitler Youth Uniform

Konrad Welker, Hilda's second oldest brother, serving in WWII

Left, friend of brother Konrad; Konrad, pictured on right, after he had suffered an injury to his face and head during battle in WWII. Konrad continued to serve in the military after a short time of recuperation.

On route to immigrate; this photo taken at Bremen Germany in front of the International Refugee Organisation office there. As Displaced persons immigrating to the U.S.A. Hilda and her family went through this office on their way to Bremerhaven Germany to board their ship, the General Muir, in 1951.

back row (left to right): Dad, Mom, youngest brother
front row (left to right): older sister, Hilda, twin, Aunt Barbara

We have arrived! Customs building on Ellis Island New York, USA, the three sisters are wearing the coats made of the fabric that Hilda's sister had woven.

back row (left to right) : youngest brother, father Ludwig
middle row (left to right): twin, older sister, Hilda
front row: mother, Luisa seated

Mother and daughter, Hilda and Dawn: still growing in faith and thanking God for His perfect Love in Christ and His Holy Spirit who leads us onward.

RESOURCES AND SELECTED BIBLIOGRAPHY

Bailey, Becky A. *I Love You Rituals*. New York: HarperCollins Publishers Inc., 2000

Collins, Larry, Dominique Lapierre. *O Jerusalem! Day by Day and Minute by Minute the Historic Struggle for Jerusalem and the Birth of Israel*. New York: Simon & Schuster, 1972

Davies, Norman. *Europe: A History*. New York: Harper Collins, 1996

DeMint, Jim, U.S. Senator. *Saving Freedom*. Nashville, Tennesee: Fidelis Books, 2009

Federer, William J. *Change to Chains: The 6,000 Year Conquest for Control Volume I—Rise of the Republic*. St. Louis, MO: Amerisearch, Inc., 2011

Feuerstein, Reuven, Rafael Feuerstein, and Louis H. Falk. *Beyond Smarter*. New York: Teachers College Press, 2010

Feuerstein, Shmuel. *Biblical and Talmudic Antecedents of Mediated Learning Experience Theory: Educational and Didactic Implications For Inter-Generational Cultural Transmission*. Israel: The International Center for the Enhancement of Learning Potential, 2002

Foster, Genevieve. *Augustus Caesar's World*. San Luis Obispo, CA: Beautiful Feet Books, 1975

Fruchtenbaum, Dr. Arnold G. *Footsteps of the Messiah*. Tustin, CA: Ariel Ministries, 2003

Ham, Ken, Greg Hall. *Already Compromised*. Green Forest, AR: Master Books, 2011

Hannaford, Carla, Ph.D. *Smart Moves: Why Learning Is Not All in Your Head*. Salt Lake City, UT: Great River Books, 2005

Hart-Davis, Adam, editorial consultant. *History: The Definitive Visual Guide, From the Dawn of Civilization to the Present Day.* New York: DK Publishing, 2007

Hedrick, Larry, ed. *Xenophon's Cyrus the Great: The Arts of Leadership and War.* New York: St. Martin's Press, 2006

Kedourie, Elie, ed. *The Jewish World: History and culture of the Jewish people.* New York: Harrison House/Harry N. Abrams, Inc., 1986

Levine, Peter A., Maggie Kline. *Trauma Through a Child's Eyes.* Berkeley, CA: North Atlantic Books, 2007

Maier, Paul L. *Josephus: The Essential Works.* Grand Rapids, MI: Kregel Publications,1994

McCullough, David. *John Adams.* New York: Simon & Schuster, 2001

McCullough, David. *1776.* New York: Simon & Schuster, 2005

North American Feuerstein Association, www. thinkingconnections.com.

Purvis, Karyn. *The Attachment Dance: How Abuse and Neglect Drive a Holocaust Problem.* Fort Worth, TX: TCU Institute of Child Development/Red Productions, 2007

Purvis, Karyn, David Cross, and Wendy Sunshine. *The Connected Child.* New York: McGraw-Hill, 2007

Rosen, Ceil and Moishe. *Christ in the Passover.* Chicago, IL: Moody Publishers, 2006

Siegel, Daniel, M.D. *The Neurobiology of We.* Boulder, CO: Mind Your Brain, Inc./Sounds True, 2008

The Commission of Children at Risk. *The Neurochemistry of Fear.* Fort Worth, TX: TCU Institute of Child Development/Red Productions, 2008

The Holy Bible, *New International Version.* Grand Rapids, MI: Zondervan Publishing House, 1994

Waring, Diana. *Ancient Civilizations and the Bible.* Petersburg, KY: Answers in Genesis, 2008

Waring, Diana. *Romans, Reformers, Revolutionaries.* Petersburg, KY: Answers in Genesis, 2008

Wikipedia. Crvenka. Internet 2012

Wikipedia. Miklos Horthy. Internet 2012

Winik, Jay. *THE GREAT UPHEAVAL America and the Birth of the Modern World, 1788–1800.* New York: HarperCollins Publishers, 2007

World Book Encyclopedia. Chicago, IL: World Book, Inc., 1989